How to Make People Do What You Want

Methods of Subtle Psychology to Read People, Persuade, and Influence Human Behavior

professional before attempting any techniques outlined in this book.

By reading this document, the reader agrees that under no circumstances is the author responsible for any losses, direct or indirect, which are incurred as a result of the use of information contained within this document, including, but not limited to, — errors, omissions, or inaccuracies

Table of Contents

Your Free Gift 1

Introduction & Foreword 3

Chapter One – Understanding The Art Of
Persuasion 9

Chapter Two – Developing Your Own Mindset 16

Chapter Three – Nurturing A Relationship 24

(Making Friends And Winning Them Over) 24

Chapter Four – Being Able To Talk To Anyone 35

Chapter Five - Deep-Diving Into Control Of
The Mind 47

Chapter Six – Mastering The Art Of Body
Language 62

Chapter Seven – The Power Of Social
Pressure 86

Chapter Eight – How Repetition Changes
Everything 103

Chapter Nine – Incentivise! Rewarding For
Results 113

Chapter Ten – The Power Of Positivity 124

Chapter Eleven – Getting Better With Practice
(Tips & Tricks) 135

Chapter Twelve – Final Thoughts...........................141

References.. 143

Your Free Gift

As a way of saying thanks for your purchase, I want to offer you a free bonus E-book called ***Bulletproof Confidence Checklist*** exclusive to the readers of this book.

To get instant access just go to:

https://theartofmastery.com/confidence/

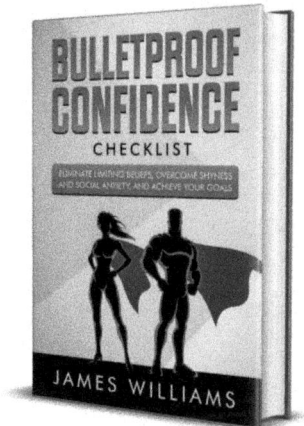

Inside the book, you will discover:

- The science and psychology of shyness & social anxiety
- Simple yet powerful strategies for overcoming social anxiety
- How to become a more confident person by developing these traits

- Traits you must DESTROY if you want to become confident
- Easy techniques you can implement TODAY to keep the conversation flowing
- Confidence checklist to ensure you're on the right path of self-development

Introduction & Foreword

"At the end of reasons, comes persuasion." – Ludwig Wittgenstein

Here's something to get your brain juices flowing.

The human race wouldn't be where it is today without communication.

The way we talk, act, and perceive ourselves, others, and the world around us is singlehandedly responsible for everything that has happened. And I mean absolutely everything. Through redemption and destruction. Through thick and thin. Both morally and immorally. The whole of society as we know it is what it is because of the effects of communication.

That's a bold statement, I know, but take a moment to think about it on a personal level. Consider every single experience that comes to mind. Every relationship you've been in. Every job you've ever loved and hated. Every chance encounter and every plan fulfilled. At every step of the way, there has been a degree of communication. Similarly, many of our professional and personal problems stem from a *luck* of communication.

In a roundabout sense, you could say communication is the key to being human, which would mean that through understanding the power that comes with mastering the art of communication, you can unlock a new way of living your life. New doors will open, and vibrant opportunities you couldn't even imagine will present themselves to you.

By mastering communication, you can achieve what only so many people dreamed of achieving.

Okay, allow me to kick it back a notch.

While this all sounds very exciting, you're probably wondering what it has to do with you and learning how to persuade people. We all persuade people in many different ways and many different forms. Many of us persuade others every day, or least are persuaded by someone else. Some people are better at it than others, just as some people are more persuadable than others.

You cannot get through life without persuading people. In your relationships, you persuade people to go on dates, get a pet, move in together, get married, and have kids. You make friends and take vacations, choose movies, and read books. Every single advertisement of any form is an attempt to persuade you to buy something.

In your professional life, you're selling to your customers, promoting and pitching your ideas to your bosses, and surviving employee evaluation meetings.

Every single aspect of human life in the modern world is affected by persuasion, or similarly, the art of influence.

But let's break this down further. Yes, people persuade other people all the time. You do it to people, and people do it to you. Understanding this, you'll soon realize that to get what you want out of life, you're going to need to persuade people. But what does this mean?

At the core of communication, there is a single thing that drives motivation for speech. It's the centre of every society, every political campaign, every message you've ever read, and every lover's proposal asked under the stars.

That single core factor is a message.

Any time you talk, ask something, share an idea (from starting a business to choosing a vacation destination), or request a favor, you're sending a message. Discussing what takeout you're going to get is sending a message. You're saying that you want pizza when your partner sends their message detailing that they want pasta.

However, choosing what takeout you have and trying to persuade your partner to get pizza over pasta is small fish to what you'll be able to achieve once you've finished with this book. Ever wanted to have your ideas listened to at work? Ever wanted to start a social movement? Ever wanted to walk into a room and actually have people listen to what you have to say in a way that isn't arrogant and egotistical, but charismatic and genuinely appealing?

This is what it means to master the art of persuasion. These are just grains of sand on the beach of what is possible. To really break this down:

You have a message to send. Sending a message is easy. Anyone can do it. I can go and stand in the street and shout for ten minutes about how pizza is so much better than pasta. That's sending a message. So is whispering it. The difficulties come when trying to get others to listen to your message.

The real art of influencing others comes with sending your message in a way that other people hear what you have to say and then actually take it on board. Getting people to listen and hear what you're saying is the message and core focus of this book. Robert Cialdini, the author of *Influencer and Pre-Suasion: A Revolutionary Way to Influence and Persuade,* once wrote:

"It's not about your message, but the skill you put into crafting it, that matters."

Never a truer word written.

By mastering the fundamentals and then the complexities of persuasion, you're harnessing your inner ability to send your message in a way that can be clearly acknowledged, received, accepted, and understood. You're enabling people to hear you and open their minds to your thoughts, concepts, and perceptions.

Let's face it: human beings these days are pretty closed off. The vast majority of people walk around all day stuck in their own minds, thoughts of stuff they read on social media and the contents of ads ricocheting off the sides of their heads. There's no doubt we live in an age where people are more polarized than ever before politically, socially, and so on.

Having the skill set to strike through the constant thinking and closed-mindedness that most people have to be genuinely heard is a lifelong skill that brings so many benefits. Within the following pages, this is a skill set I'm going to nurture within you.

We're going to be touching base with a wide range of communication techniques, including understanding NLP, learning how to read and control your body language, and applying pressure in the right places and the right time to get people to perceive what you're saying to them in a more suggestible way. We'll also cover the basics and set a foundation of human psychology and how it works, and how to send your message using these techniques.

Using these methods, you'll become far more influential in all areas of your life, both with the people you know and love, and even strangers. These are techniques that work across the board whenever you want to use them.

The book is split into chapters in such a way that it will take you on a journey. I'm going to talk you through how persuasion can be used in your day-to-day life, and eventually onto bigger ventures, as well as detailing the kind of mindset you need to carry out these skills. This is all in what is essentially a step-by-step guide to persuading an individual or group of people.

In a world of constant, high-speed communication, mastering the ability to communicate and protecting yourself from unwanted influence has never been more important.

Chapter One – Understanding the Art of Persuasion

"Think twice before you speak, because your words and influence will plant the seed of either success or failure in the mind of another." – Napoleon Hill

My interest in the art of persuasion first came to me while I was in college. I was studying business marketing, and one day my professor split the class into groups and set us to work on a project. The project was to create a marketing campaign for a new pair of Nike trainers that had just been released.

The exercise was clearly to take into account everything we had learned during the year so far and to combine it all into a concept that could sell units. I love this kind of task because it's a chance to exercise my creative side; by far, my favorite aspect of marketing. It's what I love about the world of business. The exploration of new ideas. The telling of stories. A creative process.

I went back to my dorm and brainstormed some ideas. I did some market research, watching old trainer ads and researching brands. I checked out other brands to see what they were up to at the time, and, just as I was falling to sleep, the idea hit me. There's nothing like the tingle you get when inspiration hits, and I knew right away that my idea was a winner.

The idea was this. Picture a girl getting up in the morning and putting on her Nike trainers. She leaves her house and starts running through the city. As she runs, the film would cut to shots of distractions that are symbolic in her own life. Email notifications pinging on her computer. Bosses slamming piles of reports on her desk. Shots of the busy flow of traffic. That kind of thing.

As she ran, she slowly lost herself to the running. The city and all the distractions she had in her life would fade away, and she would begin running past trees and finally into a full-blown forest. She lost herself in her running. It was her escape. It was her *freedom*. She would eventually arrive at a clearing in the woods, rain pouring down onto her, music playing through her headphones. She would savor the freedom that her trainers had helped her achieve. That *Nike* had helped her achieve. Then, refreshed and revitalized, she would run back into the city and back to her life, ready to face whatever her day threw her way.

I don't know whether Nike would have loved that idea for an ad nor any clue how successful it would have been, but I loved that idea, and I truly believed in it. I got to college the next day and sat down with the group, and I couldn't wait to share my idea. *This is it,* I thought to myself. *We've nailed this.*

We met up, went to a café in the city, and the others started listing off their ideas. There were some okay ideas, and when it got to me, I shared my idea with as much enthusiasm as I thought I could muster. I was returned blank faces, a couple of people taking notes, and then the guy to my left shared his idea. And that was it.

Now, when I was in college, I was a pretty shy kid. I had such crippling social anxiety, which was probably a key reason why my idea didn't land as impactfully as I wanted it too, but I was still heartbroken. My message—the message I had so much love and passion for—was rejected. Practically ignored.

One guy opposite me, who was easily the most charismatic of the group, shared his idea of a sports day and followed the kid growing up into an athlete. His idea was chosen, and the group ran with it. We didn't do too badly with the final result and got average marks for the project, but I was left with something far more powerful.

The day after sharing our ideas, I was left wondering what I could have done better. How could I have communicated my message more effectively? Could I have been more passionate or personal? Should I have been more dramatic or over the top? How could I have presented my ideas differently?

It wasn't until after spending many years in a career in sales and marketing and having learned about the fundamentals of human psychology and the art of persuasion that I started to learn that communicating effectively is a mastery that is learned and practiced. It's a skill that's honed over the years, not something that we just have.

Anyone can talk, but few speak value.

It doesn't matter what you want to achieve in your life; persuasion is the way you're going to make it happen. When you meet someone for the first time, and you have a romantic interest in them, you'll persuade them to spend time with you. You'll act funny or kind. You'll compliment them, or you'll act in some other way. Whatever you do, you're sending the message that "This is who I am. I like you, and I hope you like me too." If you persuade well enough, you'll go on a few dates and eventually get together. You could date for a few years and will decide to get married.

Even within the proposal of marriage itself, you're hoping you've persuaded your partner enough that they're going to say yes and will want to spend the rest of their life with you. Of course, writing about the process of love in this way makes it feel a bit robotic and not very exciting at all, but the core of what I'm saying is that you're always sending a message to other people with everything you do. If you're not in control of the message you're sending, then you'll be lucky if you get the outcome you want.

This is the purpose of this book. Persuasion is not just about getting what you want and having things your way, although you could certainly look at it that way if you wish. Instead, it's more about being in control of the messages you're sending and showing up in the world the way you want to, not just showing your face to the world and hoping for the best.

I've been that way for most of my life, and it never got me anywhere. I was always working under the people I disliked, was always the second choice for everything, and was never listened to nor barely acknowledged. It wasn't until I took control of my actions and messages that life started to swing in my favor.

I've spoken a lot about using persuasion on the personal side of life, but I can't stress enough how it extends to every part, especially from a professional standpoint. I spent many years in sales and marketing, in which the very essence of the work is persuading people to buy a product or use a service. These techniques work here in the very same way.

I take a product, no matter what it is, and send a message to a customer that says, "Buy this product, and it will make your life better in x-amount of ways." Fast food chains claim their food tastes good. Car companies sell you freedom when you drive. Clothing companies say their products will make you feel good in your own body.

It's up to you whether or not you believe in the messages these companies are selling you, but since many of these businesses are multi-million, if not billion, dollar companies, there's no denying that it works. The messages of these companies are received loud and clear.

Bringing it back to you, let's say it's time for your employee evaluation time, and you're sitting down with your boss to see how well you're doing. You're going through your figures, and they're asking you how you see yourself within the company. How confident and in control are you of the message you're sending? Will your boss want to keep you on and see you as a valuable asset within the company, or are they doubting you and your abilities? You're persuading them either way with the words you say.

Let's say you want to work for yourself, and you have an idea for a business. Whether you're pitching your idea to friends, family, colleagues, or investors, you're controlling your message to say, "This is my idea, and I want you to be on board with it." However, as Cialdini wrote, it's not about the message you're sending, it's about how you craft it that matters.

In the real world, anyone can sell you anything or influence you into believing anything. It's all about how it's presented, all of which I'm going to describe in the following chapters.

Chapter Two – Developing Your Own Mindset

"Life isn't about finding yourself. Life is about creating yourself." – George Bernard Shaw

Before you start influencing other people, it's so important to start thinking about yourself, particularly the mindset you have. When I was in college with my killer Nike trainers idea, my mindset was in the right place, but it wasn't developed enough to send a message. I suffered from crippling social anxiety and wasn't confident in myself in front of others. My message was good, but the way I crafted it and presented it wasn't.

This social anxiety created a shy, introverted "vibe" to my being. My body language screamed it, and my verbal communication confirmed it. Before I had even uttered a word, the people in my marketing group decided whether they would listen to me or not, whether they were conscious of that decision or not, and my mindset was the basis of where this decision came from.

When it comes to showing up how you want to show up in your life, taking control of the messages you're sending, and ultimately influencing others, what kind of mindset should you have to make these efforts successful? Here are some traits you need to be thinking about.

Confidence and Belief in Yourself

This mindset trait you should have goes without saying, but it's crucial and has to be mentioned. If you don't believe in yourself, and I mean truly believe in yourself, others are not going to believe in you either. Building up confidence in yourself is a process and a journey you'll need to undertake if you want to persuade people and live a happy and fulfilling life. Since you, like everybody else, change who you are as you go through life, don't be surprised that there's no endpoint where you're confident in yourself always and forever.

Your circumstances are always changing, which means you'll constantly need to be adapting your mindset to keep believing in yourself. It's a lifelong journey that you always need to be thinking about. What's more, everybody is different, so what confidence practices work for someone else may not work for you. Most of this process is trial and error, but once you start making progress, you'll start seeing unbelievable results.

By adopting a self-confident mindset, you'll already see incredible changes in the way people see you, hear you, and perceive your ideas and your messages. Fortunately, there are a few things you can do to start working towards a more confident you.

Firstly, confidence starts with you. It doesn't come from an external source. You need to start considering what limiting beliefs you have that hold you back and start letting them go. For me, my social anxiety held me back, and it made me believe on an identity level that I was not a social person. It became who I was.

In truth, this was just a belief I *gave* myself. I was full of self-doubt and never believed I was good enough, and that I never would be. As soon as I acknowledged these thoughts I held about myself and realized they existed, I was able to bring this awareness into my interactions with the world. If I wanted to share an idea and the limiting belief crept in, I could notice it and let it go, rather than being reactive to it and letting it dictate the flow of conversation.

For example, if I were in a meeting and had to give a presentation, the time would draw closer to the slot I was presenting in, and I would sit around the table thinking to myself, *Nobody's going to listen or care what I have to say.* I would notice this thought and change it. I would think something along the lines of, *No, I do believe in myself, and this presentation is going to be a hit. Even if the idea isn't chosen, I'm still going to present it to the best of my ability.*

It took some time, but eventually, my limiting beliefs were not the first point of call for my mind. Instead, I had more confident beliefs in myself, and thus I started to believe in myself fully. This confidence radiated through my conversations, and people noticeably started to respect me and treat me with authority.

This confidence that you should be building in yourself needs to be accompanied by respecting yourself. You're a human being, and you're going to make mistakes throughout your life. Instead of beating yourself up because you did something wrong, treat every negative experience positively by viewing it as a lesson to be learned.

Life is all about learning lessons, and as long as you're open to learning them, you'll always have the ability to grow as an individual. This capability to grow is how respect, confidence, and self-belief for yourself are nurtured.

Be Patient

When it comes to developing yourself within your persuasion journey, whether you're influencing someone using psychological techniques or learning to believe in yourself, patience is absolutely key.

Let's say you're trying to convince your boss to give you a promotion. You say your piece, and now the ball is in their court. This is where patience comes in. If you're constantly bothering your boss, nagging for an answer, or you're so distracted at work worrying about whether you've got the job or not, this is going to send out the message into the world that you're distracted, worried, and anxious. Well, guess what? This message won't get you the promotion!

Instead, if you're calm, collected, and patient, you're sending out the message that you're fully in control. You're relaxing to be around. You're confident that what you've said is enough (believing in yourself and your abilities), and you're giving the other people involved the opportunity to think things through and make their own decision. At least they think they're making their own decision, when actually you've persuaded them in such a way that they've already made their decision, they just don't know it yet. But more on that later.

The best way to instill patience into your life is to recognize that everything takes time. Simon Sinek once said, "You didn't fall in love with your wife the day you met her, nor five years down the line. You can't tell me the exact day you fell in love with her, but you know it was a process that happened over time."

Big things happen over time.

Be a Relationship Person

I never used to be a "people person," and unless you're super confident in yourself already, then chances are you're not either, but it's vital to be interested in relationships with people if you want to succeed with your influencing efforts. However, I'm not talking about snapping your fingers and suddenly becoming the most charismatic and charming person in the room. You still need to be yourself. I'm talking about focusing on building valuable relationships with people, no matter who you're with or what the situation is.

About five years ago, I was busy trying to secure a new client for my work. The contract was worth around $50,000, and it was one my company was paying special attention to. We wanted to approach them in just the right way that they didn't want to go with any other company, thus confirming the contract as ours. The boss was anxious because if we approached them in the wrong way, we might scare them away forever.

We didn't end up securing the contract, and looking back on the situation in hindsight, I've realized one very important lesson. My company's bosses were not interested in working with the client on a personal or even professional level. They were much more interested in chasing the instant financial gain that would come with securing the $50,000 contract. They wanted money in the bank over a partnership with the client.

I spoke to a peer from the rival company several years later, who told me they were still working with that same client. The bosses played golf together every other weekend, and the sales team knew their contacts by name and had quarterly meetings where they went to dinner as a group; employees and all.

Instead of my company chasing the money, a different way to approach would have been to communicate with the client on a personal level while aiming to build a relationship with them. Sure, we may not have secured the $50,000 leading product contract, but if we had a nurtured relationship with them, we could have secured a $20,000 contract every year for the next three years on smaller product lines, which is ultimately more profitable. Instead, we severed ties altogether.

This logic applies to both personal and professional relationships. If you focus on the value of the relationship itself, instead of what value you can get out of the relationship, you can start to persuade far more effectively. Naturally, you'll be much more likely to get more from your relationship, all without actually looking for it.

Bearing all these points in mind, you should start to form the mindset of someone capable of persuading and influencing others. It's a timely process, but with attention and effort, you should start to see the effects of a growth mindset almost instantly. Once you've created a positive relationship with yourself, it's then time to start focusing on your relationship with other people.

Chapter Three – Nurturing a Relationship
(Making Friends and Winning Them Over)

"You can make more friends in two months by becoming interested in other people than you can in two years by trying to get other people interested in you." – Dale Carnegie

In that last paragraph, I wrote about forming a mindset where you focus on creating and nurturing valuable relationships with other people and the importance of doing so when it comes to persuasion. That's a very special point because if you don't have relationships with others, you can't persuade them. This is why it's important to focus on this as a chapter of its own since it's the first step you'll take when you're starting to influence someone.

So far, you've read about persuading people, why you'd want to, and the power it can bring into your life, so you should have a pretty clear grasp on the concept. That means for the remainder of this book, I'm going to take you on a journey into how you can begin to master this fine art.

Now it's time to start taking action by controlling the messages you're sending to the world.

First, unless you're in a position of power, nobody will be persuaded or influenced by you if they don't like you. When I was a teenager, I worked in a supermarket as a shelf stacker on the weekends. It was an okay job, but my team leader was one of the worst people I had ever met. Sure, I did the work he told me to do begrudgingly, but if he called up trying to get me to fill vacant overtime slots or work an extra shift when the store was behind, there was absolutely no way I was doing it. The idea of working with him was awful, and everyone felt the same.

On my shift, I would avoid him like the plague, and would always cringe, along with everyone else, as he ranted about whatever subject was hot that day in the staff cafeteria. In contrast, there was another team leader who was simply the polar opposite. She was kind and caring, always asked how my day was, and made me feel valued as an employee—and more importantly, as a person. I know stacking shelves is not the most fulfilling job in the world, but she always made me feel appreciated for doing it. I was happy to work with her.

Whenever she called to fill an overtime shift or needed help during the busy periods, I was happy to help. I wasn't alone in this way of thinking. All the staff felt the same and treated both team leaders in the same contrasting ways, all because one team leader was liked, and the other wasn't. If you want people to do what you want, you first need to get them to like you.

There are several ways you can get in people's good books, many of which we're going to explore throughout this chapter. Remember, these points can be applied in any situation. You can apply them with your partner or someone you're working with, like a co-worker or client. You can even apply them to a stranger you've just met.

I encourage you to try these points out in any situation you can, because the more you practice them, the better and more confident you'll be at presenting yourself, thus achieving better results.

Put the Other Person First

The first step to making someone like you is to put them first in your conversations. People love to be listened to, heard, and acknowledged, and giving someone that feeling in a world where seemingly nobody is really listening is instantly going to make you stand out, and they'll remember you. This always means they'll want to speak with you again and will be much more susceptible to your persuasion attempts.

Imagine you're arguing with your partner, and you're both screaming at each other, trying to share your point of view on a particular topic. Yeah, we've all been there.

After a lot of shouting, you realize the conversation isn't going to go anywhere, and you're both going to end up driving each other away. By stepping back from this approach and putting your points of view on the back burner, and instead by listening to your partner and giving them a platform to talk, you allow progress to be made.

This may sound counterproductive, because how are you going to persuade someone if they're doing all the talking? We'll get to that later. The first thing you want to focus on is building a relationship with the person you're speaking to, getting them to connect with you positively. If other people see you as a friend, then you're heading in the right direction.

In a nutshell, let the other person do all the talking.

Listen More Than You Talk

This point goes along with everything I've already said, but the more you can listen to someone, the more connected they're going to feel to you. This doesn't just mean listening and nodding along with whatever they're talking about. It means *actively* listening and asking questions if you don't understand. It means progressing the conversation in line with what they're talking about, not just holding in what you want to say until they're finished.

Whenever I deal with a new client, I let them talk about their project in their own time. I won't say how I can help them, what my ideas are, or where I can take their product or service. I first hear their ideas and build up an image of what they're telling me.

A recent customer was trying to think of ways to market their bakery. I had some ideas, and some themes instantly come to mind, but I listened and homed in on what they were saying. When I wanted to know more, such as whether it was a family business, or what kind of market they were aiming to tap into, I wasn't afraid to ask. The act of asking questions to clarify what someone is saying is vital because it shows you're listening. It tells that person you care.

Create Trust

Trust is a key part of any relationship, and whether you're talking with a loved one you've known for years or someone who's just appeared in front of you for the first time, you need to invoke a sense of trust. If people trust you, you'll be able to influence them naturally. Nobody wants to work with a leader they can't trust. The world is already full of enough of them as it is.

There are endless ways you can encourage and nurture trust in any relationship. Firstly, you can start as simply as using the person's name in your conversations with them. Yeah, it's really that simple. Being able to make your message personal and direct to an individual already shows that you're on board with them, recognizing them as a person, and speaking to them directly. This is especially important in professional relationships.

Next, be able to admit when you're wrong, own up to your mistakes, and share any baggage you're carrying when it's necessary to do so. Everyone knows that everybody messes up from time to time. It's an inescapable fact of life. However, when most people mess up and run into problems, their first response is to try and cover everything up as best as they can. This is where lying and deceit thrive.

If you do something wrong and have the ability to own it and take responsibility for it, everyone is going to trust you from the word *go*. Let's say you're working on a project with other people, and you fill out a budget form incorrectly. It's something small, but it causes a few problems that need to be resolved. Instead of trying to shift the blame or make it look like something outside of your control happened, you simply raise your hand and admit to your shortcoming.

Suddenly, what could be quite a big problem is now not so much of a big deal. Everybody involved understands what happened and thinks, *Yes, we know what happened, and they* (being you) *weren't afraid to admit it.* Suddenly, even though you did something wrong, massive positives came from the situation because everyone saw that you were willing to own up to your mistakes in a respectful way.

Suddenly, your words have power and truth.

Work on your Body Language

We're going to discuss this topic in a lot more detail in a following chapter, but as a little introduction that ties in nicely with learning how to befriend people and get them to like you, you need to think about your body language and how people perceive you because of it. When I was a shy college student, my body was hunched over, and I would physically hide away from the main group, whether through crossing my arms or not making eye contact. Nobody paid any attention to me because my body language sent the message that I wanted to be left alone.

Of course, if you're pushing people away, nobody is going to want to approach you. Instead, you need to be inviting and welcoming with the way you act. This means smiling and acting relaxed. If you're tense, crossing your arms, or scowling at people, you're going to give off the message that you don't want to talk or connect with that person. Instead, try lowering your shoulders, smiling, and exposing your chest. But again, more on this later in the book.

Leave People Better Than You Started

As a rule of thumb, one of the best blanket statements to remember when trying to get people to like you is to always leave them in a better, happier, more thoughtful way than before. Whether you're talking to your partner, your boss, a customer, or a stranger, always aim to leave them better off than when you started interacting with them.

If you bear this concept in mind, you're going to naturally listen more and put the other person first. You're going to make them feel heard and acknowledged with what they're saying, and they're going to feel a much deeper connection with you. With this deeper connection, they're going to keep thinking about you long after the conversation has taken place, and they'll be much more likely to want to interact with you again.

Once you reach this point, you're then ready to move on with the next stage of persuading and influencing them with your message.

Be Natural

If you're focusing too much on everything you're saying and trying to implement everything you've read in this book, then your conversations are unlikely to seem natural, and this is going to put people off. Remember, when it comes to your journey into the world of persuasion, you need to start small. Master the basics first and then add to your skills over time once you feel comfortable with your foundations.

This is crucial. Imagine you're having a conversation with someone, and all you can think about is what you're doing with your body language and what message you're sending. You're probably going to end up missing what they say, and then they'll believe you're not listening to them, and it will all go down the drain. No matter what, remember to be human!

Molding Their Perceptions

In some of your relationships, you may find that becoming friends in this way is enough to get them thinking the way you think. Through the conversations you have, you may be able to convince them of your ideas and send them your messages, and they'll take them on board, perhaps even incorporating them into their way of life.

Think of persuasion in this sense. Every human being on the planet sees their own life and the world through their perceptions. These perceptions are formed by a combination of experiences—childhood upbringing, social conditioning based on parents, their educational system, geographic demographics, and the direction their life has taken.

To persuade someone is to take control of this and input your thoughts and ideas in place of what already exists there. Once you begin to mold those perceptions and those realities, it becomes easier to persuade someone with your message.

The debate about whether veganism is an effective diet choice is a fantastic example of this. If you have a hippy-styled vegan hammering away at you for hours about the benefits of veganism and why meat-eaters are so bad (thus making a meat-eater feel defensive about their own lifestyle choices), that meat-eating individual is going to shut down and won't listen. The approach is too aggressive. They'll put up mental barriers to protect themselves and their ego, and won't listen to the information discussed.

However, if this information is being presented differently, the individual may begin to change their perception. For example, if you start listening to the individual and you realize they have an interest in the environment, or are passionate about global warming and like talking about science, then you could begin introducing the scientific benefits that adopting a vegan lifestyle can bring.

If that individual was passionate about animals, you could start introducing the facts you know about the wellbeing of farmed animals, and how veganism is helping to counter the industry in terms of wellbeing. In my own experiences, a friend I knew in school grew up on a farm and was quite familiar with slaughtering animals and the sight of the human food cycle. While he cared about animals, he knew never to grow attached to them. Therefore, the animal-loving approach wouldn't sit in the same way as it would your typical animal lover.

We'll talk more about introducing these points in a later chapter, but the important thing to remember here is that you're taking the perceptions that an individual already has, and then basing your attempts to influence them off of these perceptions.

Chapter Four – Being Able to Talk to Anyone

"If you have no confidence in self, you are twice defeated in the race of life."

– Marcus Garvey

Hand in hand with the last chapter, I want to take the time to speak about the ability to talk to anyone. More specifically, this means taking the time to build up your confidence to really harness the ability to persuade and influence someone. If you're not confident with how you speak to people, the cues and techniques we talk about in the remainder of this book will not have the best possible outcome.

In line with the Robert Cialdini quote in the front of this book, it's not about the message you're sending, it's about how you craft it, which means portraying yourself confidently and with purpose. Imagine if marketing advertisements on the television "ummed" and "ahhed" with their messaging. You'd probably laugh with how silly it all seemed and definitely wouldn't take their message seriously. The same applies to you.

With all this in mind, it's worth noting that being able to speak confidently with anyone is no easy feat, especially if you're more of a shy or introverted person by nature.

Fortunately, there are ways you can overcome your fears and anxieties, and things you can do to improve your confidence when speaking to others.

Five Ways to Boost Your Self-Confidence Dramatically

While many of us admire the confidence some people have, the way they seem to control the flow of a conversation with ease and command the attention of people around them in any room they enter (be honest, we all have a friend like this), is actually something anybody can do. Most people aren't born this way, but it's picked up, learned, and practiced over time.

With that, I'm going to detail five ways you can boost your levels of confidence in yourself dramatically. Bear in mind it's not something that's going to happen overnight, but rather takes time and energy. But, if you're able to stay mindful and focused, you should start to see an improvement in your confidence fairly quickly.

1. Be Prepared for Any Situation

Being confident starts before you even enter the room. The more prepared you are for any given situation, the more confident you're going to be. Imagine two people both going into the same job interview. Person A knows everything about the company. They know the figures.

They know what job they're applying for. They know what they're doing and what's expected of them. They know the targets and the industry. They know the company's objectives, mission, and values. They know the customer base, and they know what sort of person the company is looking for. Person A has done their research and knows what to expect.

On the other hand, Person B just applied for the job, forgot they had the interview until that morning, and turns up with nothing while planning to give their pitch off the cuff. It's very clear who's got the better chances of getting the job.

Even if your preparation for heading into a conversation is thinking about a few things you're going to ask and the things you're going to say, this is better than nothing. Having some idea of what direction you want a situation to go in is great for helping you take it there, and it will mean you have some kind of structure, rather than heading into the interaction mindlessly.

That's not to say that you should plan every detail meticulously and then rigidly stick to your plan. If you're having a conversation with someone, they may ask a question that completely changes the direction of the conversation, and that's okay. You just need to be prepared for that happening. Be free and go with the flow. With this kind of mindset, it's basically impossible not to be confident.

2. Work on the Voices in Your Head

While speaking to yourself may be a traditional sign of madness, the truth is we all have a voice in our head, which is constantly talking. Nag, nag, nag. Some of the time, you'll notice it, and at others, it will be muttering away in the background somewhere. Even if you're not conscious of it, it's still there, and if you're like the majority of people, the chances are it's a negative voice.

We all have a protective, anxious voice to some degree. It's that voice that imagines all the crazy unfathomable things that are going to happen when you head into an interview or meeting. It's the voice that beats you up when you say something wrong in a conversation, even if it isn't that bad. It's that voice that tells you you're going to mess things up when you try something new.

It's impossible to be confident when you have these voices in your head, especially when you're listening to them and letting them dictate how you feel about yourself. You'll find that the people with the lowest confidence and the lowest self-esteem will have the most negative voices. It's all about being mindful of how you talk about yourself.

If you say you're not smart, not good enough, or not beautiful enough, then you're limiting yourself based on what you believe about yourself and how others view you. It's almost like a self-fulfilling prophecy. The best thing you can do is to become mindful of the voices.

Listen to what they're saying, but not by taking it on board. Instead, be an observer to your mind.

Whenever you hear negativity in your mind, say to yourself, "Oh, there's a negative thought" and replace it with a positive affirmation instead. Over time, you'll create a positive image in yourself, and thus will become more confident.

3. Don't Compare Yourself to Others

Comparison is the thief of joy, and when you compare yourself to others, you're putting yourself in a position where you're vulnerable to lowering your self-esteem and confidence. If you compare how you run to the running abilities of an Olympic runner, you're going to think you're awful at running when that probably isn't the case.

As Einstein reportedly once said, *"Everybody is a genius, but if you judge a fish by its ability to climb a tree, it will live its whole life believing it's stupid."*

When you're going about your day, be mindful of how often you're comparing yourself to others. Once you become conscious of doing this, then chances are you're going to notice you do it far more often than you originally thought. It could happen in small ways, like wishing you had a nice coat or lunch like someone else, or bigger things like having a partner like somebody else's, a house, or a job.

This is a surefire way to create dissatisfaction in your life, and you're going to be left miserable, wishing you were somebody else or living someone else's life. Of course, you're not going to be confident in yourself if this is the way you look at things.

Instead, just like being mindful of how you speak to yourself, be aware of how you compare yourself to others. If you catch yourself thinking these kinds of thoughts, then say, "Oh, I just noticed I compared myself to someone else," and then let that judgment go. Of course, there are times when comparing yourself to someone could be valuable, or even inspirational, but this will be defined on a circumstantial basis.

Ask yourself, "Does this comparison make me happy, and does it provide value in my life, or is it harming my self-esteem?" If the thought doesn't provide value, then it doesn't serve you. Instead, be accepting and grateful for who you are as an individual, and if you want to get better at something, then work at it. Don't put yourself down for not being there already.

4. Look After Yourself—Mentally and Physically

If you don't feel good about yourself, then you won't be confident in yourself. This applies to you both mentally and physically. If you have a bit of extra weight that you don't like, or you're not mentally in a good place (i.e., experiencing a sleep deficit, eating poorly, or not exercising and beating yourself up about it), then of course you're not going to be confident in who you are as an individual.

No matter who you are or what walk of life you're from, you need to make sure you're putting self-care at the top of your priority list. After all, what's the point in doing what you do if you're not looking after yourself in the best possible way? You could work yourself in the ground or eat takeout every day because it tastes good, but you know this is always going to do more harm than good in the long term.

If you look and feel good, you're going to feel confident, but how you go about this is completely up to you. Maybe you like meditating and journaling. Perhaps crystals work for you. Maybe you like unwinding in the gym, going for runs, and taking your nutrition seriously. It's completely up to you, so try out lots of things and see what works best for you.

Be compassionate with yourself, and always show yourself the love you would expect from others. Social anxiety and low self-esteem plagued me throughout my entire life, and it wasn't until I started looking after myself that these dark feelings began to lift.

5. Trust in Yourself

If you only take one of the points from this list, let it be this one. How often do you doubt your ability to do something and let the anxieties and worries play around in your mind? For me, the answer is often, or at least it used to be throughout the majority of my life until I learned to take control and to trust myself.

From when I was in school and college and then moving into the world of work, I used to always hesitate before I jumped. I remember once I had to give a presentation to a client on how we were going to market their new product line, and I was *so* nervous. I believed in my ideas, and I knew they were good, but still, something inside me made me doubt my ability to do my job.

So many times, I felt as though I would pass out due to nerves, which affected every aspect of my life. From my relationships and work to even asking someone in the store if they had a shoe in a different size, there was always a nagging voice in the back of my mind claiming I would mess it up or cause an embarrassing scene.

I was sick of feeling this way, and it shattered my confidence and self-esteem. I couldn't talk to anyone because I thought I was always going to mess it up, and people were going to look at me and judge me in a bad way. Little did I know that I was simply projecting how I felt about myself and imagining that everyone else felt the same. This just isn't true.

I can't say this enough: You **need** to start trusting yourself. Remember, you're a human being, and you're going to make mistakes. You're going to go through hard times, just like you're going to go through good times. There are plenty of lessons to be learned ahead of you, and your life will twist and turn in all directions, and that's all okay.

You're going to be doing the best you can at any given time, and as long as you're trying to do that, you've got nothing to worry about. And don't worry, your best will change from time to time. On the days you're healthy, your best will be a lot greater than the days where you're ill.

It all comes down to your mindset.

You can do a few things to actively increase trust in yourself, such as making a small commitment and then sticking to it—like saying you're going to drink water as the first thing you do every morning when you wake up. You stick to the commitment, and you start trusting yourself more and more, but there is a time element to it, so stick with it.

As with all the points above, it's all about working on yourself over time and developing an esteemed mindset towards yourself. It's an ongoing process that's going to have some amazing days and not-so-great others. As long as you're focused on walking the path you want to take, you're heading in the right direction.

How to Talk to Anyone

Let's jump forward a few months, and you've been hard at work on your confidence. You can walk into a room and hold your own. You believe in yourself, and you believe you're capable of anything you put your mind to. This is a great place to be, but now it's time to bring it to the outside world. You need to start talking with people.

And I'm not just talking about people in your immediate circles. I mean anybody. It literally could be the next person who passes you on the street. How do you do this and remain confident in a world where everyone seems to be scared of everyone else?

Simple.

First, engage the person and find out where they stand. You could ask a question of where something is or whether they could help you with something. You could just make a passing comment on whatever is happening around you. Whatever it is, try to make it interesting, but more importantly, judge their response.

What kind of mood is this person in? Are they busy or preoccupied? Are they cheerful and happy? Are they shy? Are they angry? Are they crying? Try to figure out what mood that person is in and go from there.

If someone is angry, you may want to leave them alone, or you may want to find out what's bothering them. If you can get angry with them, then you're justifying that person's anger, which is a great way to build a relationship with someone.

Let's say you see someone, and they look angry. They look like they've been crying. Immediately, you know something is going on in their life, so be concerned. If they say they've broken up with their partner because they cheated on them, you can validate their feelings and say how horrible their partner was.

Once you've engaged and you've validated this person and how they feel, then you can start building a relationship with them. So, to recap:

- First, engage the person and assess how they're feeling

- Second, validate how they're feeling

- Third, focus on building a genuine connection and relationship

Remember how, in the previous chapter, I spoke about building that trust and leaving that person better off than when you started talking to them? This applies to strangers, co-workers, relatives, and everyone in between. Being able to talk to people in this way will come with practice, so again, look for opportunities to practice, and like every skill in life, you'll get better over time.

Now, if you bear these points in mind, you'll start developing the confident mindset that's essential for persuading and influencing others. It's all about the mindset, which leads us very nicely onto the next chapter, which is all about how the human mind works. This is the best place to start when learning how you can influence, persuade, and send your message out into the world.

Chapter Five - Deep-Diving into Control of the Mind

"The power of persuasion would be the greatest superpower of all time." – Jenny Mollen

A person's mindset is the most powerful attribute to their character and who they are, as your mindset is to yours. It doesn't matter what the physical reality is for someone; their mindset will dictate everything. If they feel defeated, they are defeated, for example.

I was watching a documentary the other night that detailed the struggles of people living in Africa. Some people were so far below the poverty line that they had to dig for scraps, mainly grains of rice and corn, that had been left on the ground outside of rat holes by the rodents that lived in them. Some days, that was those people's main source of food. Yet, despite their despair, the people were hopeful that better days were coming. They worked hard to provide a brighter future for their children and their children's children.

In the same hour, I spoke to a friend who has been in a rut the past few months. He quit his full-time job to make money on the stock exchange as a day trader but had practically lost all his investment. He's not a bad investor and had only invested his budget, meaning he still had his house and his car and his savings to support his family. Yet, he felt utterly defeated and was struggling to find a way forward.

This is the power of mindsets.

When it comes to learning how to tap into other people's mindsets, granting you an understanding of how their mind works and how you can then begin to alter their perceptions, there are three main subjects you need to think about. Schemas. Priming. Spreading Activation. Allow me to explain.

An Introduction to Schemas

Simply put, schemas are the associations that you have with the world and are, therefore, responsible for the majority of your perceptions. They were first coined by Jean Piaget, a developmental psychologist, back in 1923. There are plenty of examples to consider, most of which come in the form of stereotypes. A really basic example comes in the form of a child and their perception of a cat.

The child is living at home and frequently sees the four legs and the fur and thinks, *Yes, this is a cat.*

This perception of what a cat is is that child's *cat* schema. When the child then goes to a zoo and sees a lion, the associated cat schema is activated. Sure, both cats and lions have a lot in common, but a house cat doesn't roar, hunt wild food, and has a different body size. Once the differences have been made, the child will develop a *lion* schema to sit alongside the *cat* schema.

Schemas are created within us to hold our perceptions of the world—to give us an understanding of the world around us. These schemas can include anything from objects, social situations, and events to people, their perspectives of themselves, and their roles in life (such as within a family, a relationship, and a place of work). Others' roles and expectations are also considered, such as a schema that says waiters in a restaurant will be warm, friendly, and welcoming.

These schemas that are created based on how we view the world can be formed at any time, but—and this is the most important point—they can also be modified at any time, just as the child's cat schema was modified when they learned about the lion for the first time. With this in mind, there are two main ways a schema can be formed:

1. A schema can be created with the introduction of new information, thus being able to perceive something new with new clarity and understanding.

2. A new schema can be created by adjusting an old schema based on new information received, or

by creating a brand new one because the new information doesn't fit an existing schema.

Let's say you're talking to a friend about political parties, and you want to vote left, and they want to vote right. You both have different experiences within your lives and varying political opinions. This means your political schemas are different. If you can change someone's schema, then you'll be able to change their mind, thus persuading them to be able to vote in a different way.

The real question is, how do you trigger this process of developing or adjusting a schema, whether altering one or creating a new one entirely? The answer lies in priming.

An Introduction to Priming

Priming is a term that simply describes the process of activating a schema. When the child saw the lion, their cat schema was activated and brought from their subconsciousness into their consciousness for thought to take place. Take a moment to think about your bank account and your current financial status. You could be financially secure, or you may be in debt. You have schemas about both ways of living, and me asking you to think about it brought whichever schema is relevant to you to the front of your mind.

You may have also thought about being very wealthy or very in debt, both of which you also have a schema for. The statement of me asking you to think about your bank account is an example of priming. But what's the purpose of priming? Well, interestingly, it affects your behavior. Dramatically.

A popular study carried out by Bargh, Chen, and Burrows (1996) showed people relating various words to elderly people, such as "wise," "Bingo," "retired," etc. The study found that people who had been primed with elderly-related words then walked slower after they had been primed with said words, much in the way that elderly people do.

Simply putting the words in someone's mind was enough to change their behavior in a way that related to the words spoken. Spooky, right?

Another study published in *Aging and Mental Health* found that priming people with negatively orientated words and stereotypes negatively affected the individuals who were being primed with the words. This included effects such as increased attempts to seek help and increased loneliness.

This means that if you give someone the mental image of a lonely and fragile elderly person using the words you say, this can make people feel lonelier and more fragile. You're changing someone's behavior and mindset using only your words.

You've perhaps witnessed this in your own life. When someone mentions running water or food, you may feel the need to go to the toilet or feel hungry. The actions, words, and situations around you are priming you and your behavior. When you think about life in this way, you realize the human mind is quite simple in many ways. It's just looking for patterns in its immediate environment.

This is very common in people who have PTSD. American military vets can feel startled, their bodies physically going into shock when they hear loud bangs that resemble the sounds of gunshots and explosions from their tours in service.

When it comes to mastering the art of persuasion, you must learn about how effective priming is in the way you speak. For example, if you're persuading a client to buy into your web development package, you may talk about Facebook, Twitter, or other successful websites related to your client's niche that will prime their schemas into thinking about successful websites and then relating this thought pattern with you and your pitch.

However, we have one more stop to think about that brings this all together.

An Introduction to Spreading Activation

Spreading activation is a much more scientifically in-depth way of looking at persuasion, so I'm going to break it down as easily as possible. You have your brain. Your brain is physically made as a semantic network. It's like a spiderweb with lots of different sections and nodes that contain all the knowledge that you know. Each concept or thought or idea you know has its own individual node. Think of it like a spider's web full of raindrops, each raindrop being a node.

If I say "pets," all the nodes related to common pets related to you and your life experiences will light up. You might start thinking about cats, dogs, and hamsters. If you had some unusual pets, you might think about parrots or guinea pigs. If you grew up on a farm, you might think of pigs and cows being your pets. The point is, the priming words of "pets" lights up a node in your brain, and what lights up per priming term will be different, depending on who you are and your own life experiences.

When you think of certain pets, this inevitably lights up other parts of your mind and other related nodes, and this process is known as spreading activation, as coined by Collins and Loftus in 1975. A simple example of this could be the term "color."

You start thinking about colors: blue, green, yellow, red, etc. With red, you may then think of fire, roses, flowers, fire engines, trucks, cars, city roads, and so on. Simply from the color red, this whole network of nodes has lit up. A stream of thought is created from just a single concept. But you're probably wondering, why is this important when it comes to persuasion?

If we'd been having a conversation, and we've been talking about sunsets and flowers and fires and roses, your mind could be very primed. If I asked you to pick a color, you're more than likely going to pick red because of the previous topics of conversation.

This is mind control at its core. It may seem limited for now, but with practice and experience, this can go a long way and create some powerful effects.

This approach also works as a popular children's game where they can guess what you're thinking.

Think of a type of juice. Think of a fruit. Think of a color. Now think of a vegetable. Were you thinking carrot? It's a really simple technique, but once you've mastered it on a basic level, you can start doing some incredible things with it. While this works for kids, it may take a little more to work on adults.

A Strategy for Persuasion Using Mind Control

This kind of persuasive influence is very common among magicians. Performers will drop subtle words into a conversation that will then influence their audience to think in a certain way, usually towards a word that they wrote down as a prediction before the show even started. The audience member was always going to pick that word because the magician persuaded them through subtle clues to choose it.

When using this approach in your conversations and interactions with people, you have a lot of options to think about. Firstly, you need to think about priming the person. Let's say someone is having a bad day. They're in a bad mood, a family member or pet has passed away, or they feel like they're about to lose their job. Your goal is trying to sell them your idea for a business you have.

Trying to communicate with them about something so positive and inspiring during the negative time they're having is the worst idea because they're going to associate the meeting and conversation you have with the dark and depressing feelings they had that day. On the other hand, talking to them about such a positive idea when they're in a good mood will connect the dots in their mind of your idea being a good thing, thus making it far more likely they're going to get involved. And this is simply through choosing the right time to talk.

If you're taking into account everything we spoke about in the previous chapter about making friends and building relationships with people, then you're going to know when the best times for approaching a person is.

I've spoken a lot about the art of persuading is all about sending a message, and you're always going to want to send that message in the best possible way and at the best possible time for the best possible reception.

When you've decided there's an appropriate time to talk, focus on which schema(s) you're going to bring up. Going back to the example that you have a business idea you want to share with someone, you could talk about new beginnings and getting involved in new projects. You could talk about how starting a new chapter in life can lead to great things. Perhaps drop in a story of how you or someone you know is starting a new chapter in their life.

Just using these terms is priming the person you're speaking to, to start thinking about new chapters and new beginnings. Thanks to spreading activation, this will activate other nodes. Keep listening closely to what the other person is talking about, because you'll be able to get a glimpse into what these other nodes are, ultimately providing you with more information about which direction you can prime in.

Let's say you've spoken about new beginnings and trying new things, and you know the person is in a good mood. You may start speaking about the concept of hard work and how rewarding it is to put your all into a project. It's such a good feeling, right?

In this part of the persuasion process, you should never lie to get what you want or push the conversation in a direction that isn't true, and unless you're pro at mastering communication, your body language and the way you're speaking is going to give you away, even if that's on an unconscious level. Always stick to the truth, be genuine, and focus on developing true and honest relationships.

After several conversations (depending on what you're trying to achieve), you can start introducing the idea you're trying to influence that person on; in this case, your business idea. They'll be so primed at this point, they'll be open to the idea that you won't have to do much else.

The Mind Control Art of NLP

There's no way I could write a chapter on controlling the mind without mentioning a communication technique known as NLP. NLP, or Neuro-Linguistic Programming, is known as a psychological technique for controlling the minds of other people, although the reality is that the practice isn't that ominous. It is revered by many to have destructive potential in the wrong hands due to just how powerful it really is, but mainly it can be used to bring so much good into the world.

The majority of people who use it are therapists, counselors, and psychologists who treat patients who suffer from traumas, PTSD, stress, low confidence, low self-esteem, etc. NLP has been used in various situations and environments, although the studies have been small in scale and produced varied results.

For example, paying attention to someone and their body language (more of which I'll speak about in the next chapter) can reveal a lot of what they're thinking about. If you ask someone to think of their house and they look up to the top right or left corner of their eye, this means they're thinking of their house visually. By noticing this kind of body language, you can then continue the conversation in a visual way that will make what you're saying more appealing.

Using techniques like this, you're able to form a connection with the person you're speaking to because you'll be highlighting what resonates in what you say and what doesn't, and then furthering the conversation in the same best possible way.

NLP is also not just about listening but always about focusing on how you craft your message. Can you see or feel about the following questions,

- Let's go and have another drink.

- Do you want another drink?

Of course, the latter is a question, which means you've enabled the person you're talking with to have a choice in the matter, unlike the first statement. Not only are you giving the illusion that the other person is in control because you're not going to ask if you don't want one, but you're using words like "want." The other person is now thinking, *Hmmm, I want a drink,* and the brain interprets this by saying, "Yes, I want a drink."

If you were with a client and wanted them to have a good time and think about an offer while you were drinking, this is how you could easily persuade them to have another drink. Another fantastic example of this is when a waiter comes over and asks, "What would you like to start with?" which instantly gets you to look over at the menu. It's all about the wording and the image this creates in the person's mind.

The waiter asks what you're starting with, your brain asks the same question and starts looking at the menu and looking for food options. It's simple mind control, but it's mind control nonetheless. Let's take it a step further.

Look at these two sentences:

- My son is very good at his job, but he's not great at turning up on time.

- My son is not great at turning up on time, but he's very good at his job.

How you create a sentence using the word "but" as the foundation massively changes how the sentence sounds and is received. Even changing your wording in such a way can make a huge difference in someone's perspective towards something. In this case, the father could be trying to get his son a job in which the second sentence would be the obvious choice for the most positive results.

In the same way, there are plenty of other ways you can use NLP techniques to bring yourself closer to the person you're speaking with, ultimately giving you the connection that can help you persuade and influence them just that little bit more.

Control the Tempo of Your Voice

Mimicking the beat of the human heart with the tempo of your voice is a very common NLP technique that helps you connect. This is known as talking to the "suggestive frequency of the human mind." The average human heart tends to beat between 50 and 80 beats per minute, so aim for this. However, if you're in a particularly calm situation, you may want to be slower. Think soothing a child to help them sleep kind of slow.

On the other hand, if you're in a tense situation where heart rates are high, speaking quickly and powerfully could be the best way to communicate and deliver the best results.

Use Hot Words

Using hot words, or buzzwords, refers to visual trigger words that NLP professionals will use to get their subjects into a more susceptible mindset. When you say phrases such as hear this, see this, feel free, now, because, and smell that, you're instantly tapping into a particular sense, thus putting your subject's mind into a state where that sense is going to be at the forefront.

This is a powerful way to help you send a message.

It's worth bearing in mind that NLP is a route you can take, and there is lots to learn. To master the profession will require a lot of training and practice, so it's well worth looking into a course of sorts if it's something that interests you. When it comes to the art of persuasion, however, there are other simpler methods and practices you can use, one of the most important of which we're going to be talking about in the next chapter.

Chapter Six – Mastering the Art of Body Language

"If you want to find the truth, do not listen to the words coming to you. Rather see the body language of the speaker. It speaks the fact not audible." – Bhavesh Chhatbar

We've already covered body language a lot in the previous chapters, and that's because it's such an important point. Phew, I can hear you thinking, *It's about time!* You've probably heard of the saying that 90% of all communication is non-verbal and body language, and while that urban myth is a little extreme, the actual number is around 58%. When you consider verbal communication around 38%, you still see how important body language is when communicating a message.

Okay, making that a bit more realistic, if you're trying to get a job at a new business and you've gone into the interview, how do you think you should present yourself? If you're slouched back in the chair with your arms folded while staring at the employer, it doesn't matter what answers you give or what experience you have, you're not going to get the job.

Body language is big business. It says so much. Whether you're reading books and articles on relationships, sales, marketing, or self-help, there will be sections and chapters dedicated to body language. The point is, your body language is sending out a message to everyone around you, and it works both ways. The body language of those around you is telling you messages about them if you know what to look for and how to read the signs.

Every facial expression, every movement of the body, and every position of your hands is telling people what's going on. If you're sitting closed up and reserved and biting your nails while avoiding eye contact, you're giving away the impression you're nervous and on edge. If you walk into a room big and broad, making eye contact and smiling at everyone you pass, you give the impression you're completely at ease.

This extends into the tone and volume of your voice, the way you're standing, the amount of eye contact you give each person, and your overall posture. When you control your body language and read the body language of others, this puts you in a prime position to influence others effectively.

When it comes to body language, there's a vast library of information out there to explore, but when specifically focusing on persuading and influencing people, there's one key aspect you'll want to be thinking about known as **embodied cognition**.

Embodied cognition is all about defining the link between the mind and the body, exploring how the two are connected, and how one influences the other. It is how your mind controls the body, in all the ways you would expect, but also how the body controls the mind in the opposite direction. Think about how leaning your elbow on a desk with your head in your hand acts as and signifies that you're bored. Even when you're not bored, doing this action can make you feel bored, thus triggering a mental, and ultimately physical, response.

This appears throughout our lives. Making a fist is associated with being violent, aggressive, and assertive. Writing down negative thoughts you have about yourself can solidify them in your mind if you write them down in your dominant hand, but can oppositely affect you less if you write them with your non-dominant hand. This is the power of embodied cognition.

So, how to use this to influence?

In 1988, Strack, Martin, and Stepper conducted a study where they asked two groups of people to hold pens in their mouths. One group was asked to hold the pen in their lips, while the other was asked to bite on it. Both groups then looked through cartoon sketches and rated how funny they were. The group who were asked to bite the pens, thus putting their mouths into a natural smiling position, found the cartoons most amusing.

This is an effect known as the Facial Feedback Hypothesis. Robert Zajonc researched this theory back in 1989 and found that the body language we make can physically trigger biological responses within our bodies. You know when you're feeling sad, and people say fake a smile because it will make you feel better—the fake it 'til you make it kind of an attitude? That's what he discovered.

Within his research, he asked German students to repeat vowel sounds (a, e, i, o, u) and found that when students said "e" and "ah," it made them make smiling expressions. Try it for yourself now. On a biological level, making these expressions cooled the blood in the students' arteries, therefore lowering the brain temperature and making the students' experience a more pleasant mood.

On the other hand, he found that making the "u" sound caused a frowning expression, which caused the opposite effects. The frown raised brain temperature and decreased blood flow, causing a more negative-slanting mood. This effect can work when you use body language on yourself and others.

Applying Body Language as a Persuasive Strategy

Imagine you're talking to me about a hobby you enjoy. It could be sports, food, travel, lifestyle, or anything you want. You're telling me the details of your passion and describing above average detail. As you speak, I'm nodding my head. What do you feel? What is my body language communicating to you?

Since in the vast majority of cultures the act of "head-nodding" is a sign of agreement and open-mindedness if I nod my head at what you're saying indicates that I'm on the same page as you. I'm listening. I understand. I'm following. I want you to carry on. My act of head nodding is a non-verbal cue that tells you all of this subconsciously without me saying a word.

Take control of this act to send a message. When you're speaking to someone, and you're going to ask someone to do something, for a favor, or you're wanting to influence them with information, start bringing head nodding into your conversation. Since this has such a strong tie with the concept of agreement and understanding, you're encouraging a more agreeable statement of mind.

So, once you've made a request or shared information with someone, how can you make them agree? How can you bring the head-nodding action out of someone else? Simple. You use more body language.

When you're speaking to someone, there are naturally going to be points in any conversation where someone will acknowledge what the other person is saying. Verbally, this will sound like someone saying "uh-huh" or "yes," showing their agreement. That's the verbal parallel to a head nod. However, to trigger these acknowledgment cues, you need to create these natural pauses.

Using body language, you can do this by physically pausing what you're saying for a minute, but not too long because you don't want to disrupt the flow and momentum of what you're saying. Alternatively, you can raise your eyebrows, another non-verbal cue that you're looking for acknowledgment. This all happens within a second or so and happens so subconsciously that nobody is going to notice you doing it.

When you're in a conversation with someone, as you're building up to your request, start implementing these non-verbal cues into your body language to prime the person's mind into an agreement. Once they've agreed several times, you then share your request, and the person is far more likely to agree, which will be showcased as a visual head nod response.

Other Body Language Cues

In truth, every aspect of body language is saying something, but being aware of the core body language attributes, you can start to control them, thus controlling the message you're sending out to the world and the people around you. Remember what we said earlier about someone being defeated? What do you imagine? Someone bent or hunched over, the weight of the world on their back. This is the physical representation of someone being defeated.

Hand in hand with the persuasive head nodding and pausing cues above, let's take a moment to explore other body language cues that send a message. With awareness of these cues, you can control them how you wish, ultimately sending the message you want to send.

The Power of Posture

Posture is such a massive message sending form of body language. When someone walks into a room with their head held high, their body exposed, and their back straight, they ooze power and status wherever they go. People instantly respect people in this way because they are exposing themselves in a way that shows no fear. It shows confidence and authority. This person is meant to be here, and they feel comfortable doing it.

On the other hand, a slumped position, hunched over, or hiding certain parts of your body, such as your hands or chest, sends the impression you're anxious or nervous. Try it now, and you'll see the effect on yourself. Sit up straight, push your shoulders down, and hold your head high. Feels powerful, right?

Now slump your back, and hold your hands in your lap, hiding them between your legs. Look at the ground and never above the horizon. Feels weak and defeated, right? Even moving and positioning yourself in this way is having an effect on you and how you feel, and you're aware you're doing it, so now imagine what kind of subconscious messages you're sending out to those around you.

When applied to a conversation where you're trying to persuade someone, use your posture accordingly. If you're trying to convey authority to get somebody to listen to you, hold a high position that presents power and confidence. Likewise, when you strike this posture, you may see the other person physically backing down and slumping, which means they're feeling anxious and defeated in your presence.

When influencing someone, you don't want them to shut down completely, but instead respect what you're saying, so you don't want to go all the way. Just find the balance with each person you're speaking to on an individual level. On the other hand, you may want to empower and make someone feel good about themselves, in which case slumping back yourself may be the sign they need to feel powerful and believe in themselves.

It's all about finding what works in any given situation, depending on the outcome you want to achieve.

The Message Sent With the Eyes

We all know that eye contact is an important part of communication, and if you're speaking to someone who's looking everywhere else but at you, this sends the message that they're not there with you. Of course, depending on the circumstances of the individual situation, this can mean different things.

It could indicate boredom or distraction, or they may be shy or nervous about speaking with you. Aligned with this, where you're looking with your eyes as you converse will say a lot about you, but always on an unconscious level. Watch any street magician on YouTube, David Blaine being a prime example.

Watch how he always maintains eye contact with the people he's performing too. He directs such a strong and powerful message and influences the people he's performing because he maintains such a strong connection with his eyes.

A long story short; eye contact is direct and connecting, and powerful for sending a message. Eye contact makes people listen, feel included, and feel a part of a conversation. A lack of eye contact creates the opposite effect. How can you apply this knowledge in your conversations? Well, think about the macro of your speech.

When you're thinking about what you're saying, chances are you tend to look away. Everybody does. When you're umming and ahhing, you'll look to the side or at your feet while trying to find the words to say. This breaking of eye contact detracts from your message, and it ultimately has much less impact and power.

If, however, you take a moment to think about what you're saying before you speak, and then share your message while making full eye contact, then your message will retain its full power and impact. As the saying goes, always think before you speak. Eye contact also increases the perception of trust, whereas speaking without contact can seem suspicious and deceitful, so bear these in mind.

Exposure of Your Chest

This may seem like a strange point to consider, because I'm not talking about undoing the buttons of your shirt and exposing your chest in the literal sense, but more in the sense that your chest and how open it is is a clear body language sign that details how vulnerable someone is, and a whole lot more than that.

When I was a child, I used to play cops and robbers with my friends. I would always play the robber because my friend has a proper kids-play police outfit, and he would always run around the big tree in the back garden and shout, "Put your hands up!"

Of course, as anybody would and still do, even in real-time situations, people raise their hands and expose their chest, but what message is this sending? Well, think of it in the opposite manner. When you cross your hands in front of your chest or hold something up against it, what message are you sending now?

In most cultures and societies around the world, crossed arms and covering your chest is a sign of self-defense. If I stand up and give a speech in a meeting and sit back down and cross my arms, I'm negating any chance for people to ask questions. When someone is sat with their arms crossed, they're defensive and protecting themselves from external harm.

Use this information wisely. If you need a favor from someone, when's the best time to ask? When they are open and free to do something, or when they have something in their hands, and their arms are crossed? Clearly, the first option is best. If you can get your timing right, you'll see far more success with your persuasion efforts.

Cutting Off Your Message Before It's Over

Have you ever watched an advertisement and it seems to glitch right at the end? Like it gets cut off abruptly, only by a second or so, but it feels blunt and unfinished? This is actually a psychological tactic to help people remember what you previously said, far more effectively than if you carried on.

If you head over to YouTube, hit the Music channel, and listen to any song for several seconds and then close the tab, you're going to remember that song for the rest of the day. Guaranteed. It's because you heard a snippet of information, and your brain is thinking, *Okay, well now I want to know more.* It feels unfinished, and the mind is eager to fill in the gaps, thus holding onto everything else that has been said before.

Oppositely, if someone is talking to you sentence after sentence, and they're just going on and on and repeating the same points, you're going to get bored, switch off, and forget everything.

Applying this tactic to your own conversation, if you're detailing points to someone, share your first point, and your second point, and then it looks like you're going to share a third point, but don't. See how it makes you...

Exactly. Stopping yourself in this way abruptly stops the flow, which engages the mind in such a way that it cements the information. Of course, I'm not saying be rude with what you're saying and just stop mid-sentence and walk off, but instead use body language cues, like opening your mouth, to fake continuing. This is a fantastic tactic when you want someone to remember what you're saying.

Gestures and Hand Movements

Hand gestures are known for being able to communicate so much in such small actions. If I wave, I'm saying hello or goodbye. A more energetic version of this movement would be to try and grab your attention. If I raise my hands horizontally, palms facing down, and pat the air, I'm telling you to be quiet and settle down.

This is all basic stuff, but it's still a very important form of body language, so we have to cover it. Let's go through this rapidly. As you read through, try mimicking the gestures to see how they make you feel, what they look like to do, and then imprinting them so you can see them in other people.

- **Touch**

While I don't recommend touching everyone you meet, touching in some ways is a very powerful way to connect with other people. Even just a touch on someone's arm or shoulder can connect you to them, and it displays signs of comfort, warmth, and connection.

Be careful with how you touch people, though. If you touch with just your fingertips, this can make people very uncomfortable, and it shows you're nervous but trying to hide it. When you agree with someone, placing a firm hand on their shoulder can amplify your acknowledgments.

When touching or being touched by someone, you can also tell their state of mind and being by the temperature of their hands. Warm hands mean they are comfortable and positive, whereas cold hands may indicate tenseness and anxiety, but of course, the temperature of the room can play a big part in this.

- **Hand on Heart**

If you want to invoke feelings of trust in another person, placing your hand on your heart is a great way to do so. Hence the saying "hand on my heart," which means you can trust me or insinuates you are saying, "I promise." It means, "Believe what I'm saying or accept what I'm telling you."

- **Pointing**

Pointing can mean a lot of things. If I point at you during a conversation, it's a very imposing and authoritative gesture. Teachers and parents will point at their children when telling them off, almost as though it's directing the words of discipline they're saying directly at the children and their being.

This gesture amplifies your ability to talk down to someone and is often interpreted as angry, aggressive, and even violent. If you jab your finger, a more vigorous point, this is deemed very aggressive. As a whole, pointing is deemed impolite by most people and cultures.

However, depending on the situation, if you point with a wink or in a playful way, it can be a very empowering gesture to the person being pointed at. They can feel acknowledged and recognized, like saying, "You're the man!" when they've done a good job. It's all about the body language that accompanies the point and the context of the conversation.

- **Palms Up**

Just like exposing your chest, palms facing up is usually a very positive sign that means openness, readiness, and trustworthiness. Opening your entire arms up with upward-facing palms can be empowering and enlightening, but you can also say you don't know by shrugging your shoulders with your hands up.

However, this isn't a sign of weakness, but more a sign saying, "I don't know, but I'm comfortable enough, confident enough, and ready enough to admit that."

- **Palms Down**

With your palms facing down, you're saying you believe in what you're saying, and you're confident with your stand. This may be viewed with authority and trust, but it can also mean defiance, as though saying, "I'm not going to budge, and you can't change my mind."

- **Hands on Hips**

While there is a common idea that placing your hands on your hips can be a sign that you're unready to partake in something, or sometimes even frustration or irritated, it is much more commonly a sign that someone is ready to take action. That's why you'll see it all the time in athletes and work-lovers.

Sure, you will also see it in authority figures, such as police, military generals, and others in charge as a way of displaying assertiveness, but this still shows the individual is ready to take action.

- **Fists**

A very powerful gesture, a clenched fist is all about resolution and determination. It can be seen as violent, depending on the context of a situation, but mainly showcases an unwillingness to back down. Think about when a sports team scores and the fans will raise their fists in triumph, not unlike when a business secures a big contract after fighting for it for a long time.

If someone has made a fist with their thumb hidden in their hands, this can be a sign of anxiousness, as though the person is hardening themselves for what is to come.

- **Hand Chops**

When someone chops their hands through the air, it's a power move saying, "This is what I'm saying. I've made up my mind. Nobody can change that." It's a very definitive and authoritative move. You'll see politicians and CEOs using this gesture a lot.

- **Hands Rubbing Together**

This is a gesture that represents excitement for the future, reward, and happy times ahead. When someone places a large bet on odds that are massively stacked in their favor, this is the hand gesture that comes to mind. It's all about channeling the stress and excitement that comes from an upcoming positive situation, as well as preparing themselves for it.

- **Hands in Pockets**

Hands in pockets is usually a powerful sign that there is a reluctance to do something or an unwillingness to proceed. If you're talking to someone and they put their hands in their pockets, this shows you've lost their interest, or their mind is elsewhere.

This can also be a sign that someone is hiding the truth since hand signals can give away the truth, and they're hiding the ability to show this.

• Hands Behind Back

As we spoke about with regard to exposing your chest and keeping it open, placing your hands behind your back is a sign of confidence and comfort. Of course, it's always more trustworthy to show your hands in a situation, but if the level of trust is already there, perhaps if you're around colleagues, friends, and family members, then you may not need to do this.

Even if you're with strangers, having your hands behind your back can showcase signs of confidence and comfort. You're saying, "Here I am, and I am vulnerable," but in a controlled sense.

• Steepling

Steepling is the term given to an individual who places their fingertips together without their palms touching. This is a massive display of power, which is why you see it with evil villains in movies, chess players who are contemplating moves, or lawyers. This move is all about confidence, especially self-confidence and assurance in the future.

If you saw someone doing this in a board meeting, you can read that they truly believe they know what you're doing, and they've got some powerful information related to what's being said.

• Squeezing or Clasping Hands Together

When someone squeezes their hands together, either their entire hand or their fingers, this is a sign that someone is uncomfortable, nervous, or anxious about the situation they're in. This move is all about self-settling and trying to ground themselves. It's like a comfort gesture people give to themselves to try and make themselves feel better.

Sometimes people will rub their wrists, and this is the same sign. When you spot this in someone or yourself, you may need to comfort that person, empower them, or there's an opportunity to find out what's going on.

Reading the Body Language of Others

While there is a whole range of benefits that come with controlling your own body language in any given situation, remember, it's not all about controlling your own language, but also reading the language of others. Let's take a trip back in time to the previous chapter, where we were talking about making friends with people. You're talking to a stranger and have just started a conversation, perhaps over the water cooler at the office.

The individual is talking and making a lot of eye contact, they're making wild hand gestures as they speak, and their chest is open, almost inviting you in. What is this body language communicating? It's saying, *I'm happy in this conversation. I'm engaged. I'm connected to you.* This is a conversation I'm enjoying being a part of.

This shows you that the person is probably in a positive mood, having a good day, and is more likely to be agreeable and open with what you're saying. If you needed to ask a favor, this is a good person to engage with.

On the other hand, if someone is leaning against the water cooler and not looking at anyone, is blunt with their responses, and has their arms crossed, this says the complete opposite to the example above. Use this information wisely when choosing how to approach a situation and deal with certain people, finally allowing you to determine the best approach to influencing someone.

Mirroring Someone's Body Language

You may have already heard about mirroring the body language of others and the power that comes with that, but there's a fine line when it comes to using the art of mirroring properly. If you mirror someone exactly, movement to movement, this is just plainly obvious, and it's going to make the other person feel uncomfortable.

However, mirroring in the right way, with just the right amount of mirroring, you can connect far deeper than you normally would with even a complete stranger. This has been proven in endless studies, including Val Barren 2003, where waitresses made higher tips, and in Gueguen, Martin, and Meineri in 2011, where students convinced other students to write their essays for them.

Mirroring is a fantastic way to persuade someone and influence them to do something because it makes the other person feel way more at ease and connected. Because they're already doing the body movements and gestures and now, you're doing them on a subconscious level, they believe that everything is being acknowledged and accepted, providing complete comfort and a state of mind, which is much more agreeable.

There are four main steps you can follow if you want to mirror someone properly.

Step One

Start by fronting the person you're speaking with, which means being with them and giving them your full attention. Put them in front of you and make them everything to you at that moment. Give them full eye contact and nod when they speak. Roughly, nod three times when agreeing to really drive home your acknowledgment.

You can boost this further with a bit of imagination. For a moment while they're speaking, pretend they are the most important person in the world, even just for a second or two, and then stop pretending and return to giving them your full attention. Even in these few seconds, you'll send all the non-verbal cues that make them feel like, to you, nothing else but them matters.

Step Two

Start mirroring their actions. If they sit back in their chair and slump, wait a few seconds and do the same. If the other person starts speaking faster or louder, slower and quieter, then do the same. The two main things to remember here is matching their pace and their volume.

Step Three

Find their punctuator. A punctuator is the non-verbal cue or tell which the person will do every time they make a point and display the tell to clarify that point. A common one is tipping their head forwards and perhaps raising an eyebrow. Another common one is using a hand gesture, like the chopping or pointing we spoke about above.

Find the punctuator and start mirroring it!

Step Four

Okay, at this point, you and the person you're speaking to should already feel a strong connection, and they should already be in an agreeable state of mind, which makes this step optional, but if you really want to see how strong the connection is, then test it for yourself.

The easiest way to do this is to take any action that is unrelated to the conversation so far and then see if they mirror it back. If you've gone out for a drink, you may take a sip, or even just move your glass randomly to another nearby point on the table. If they mirror and do the same, you know your connection is strong!

One final point to remember is to ensure you're only mirroring the positive actions and cues the person is giving you. If someone picks up their phone, or is distracted and looks away, or sits with their arms folded with their chest closed off, don't mirror these actions. Instead, remain patient, keep mirroring the positives, and you'll see the connection forming.

When it comes to body language aligned with the art of persuasion, changing the way you act and stand isn't going to be the be-all and end-all strategy that will influence people to do what you want while controlling their behavior.

However, when applied alongside the other strategies in this book, and when it comes to reading the situation and person and defining what approach you're going to take, the body language strategies you've learned here are invaluable. This applies in both individual and group settings, the latter of which we're going to explore in the following chapter.

Chapter Seven – The Power of Social Pressure

"As much as people refuse to believe it, the company you keep does have an impact and influence on your choices." – Unknown.

It doesn't matter what book, article, or video you watch on persuasion—social pressure is always going to be a part of it. It's nearly the most important form of persuasion, as well as being one of the most powerful. You'll be absolutely amazed at the ways that social pressure can affect and influence the behavior of an individual.

Think about how children are subject to social pressure, in particular, peer pressure, throughout their lives. If a teenager is hanging out with a group of teenagers who are all smoking, even if the teenager in question is against smoking, if offered a cigarette when everyone else is doing it, then they're more likely to do it.

This effect follows everyone throughout their entire lives, from the time they are children to the day they die. Social pressure is enormous, and it's vital for you to understand the power it has.

Within the sections of this chapter, we're going to explore the intricacies of social pressure, allowing you to understand the psychology of this theory, and then how to control this pressure and weave it such a way that you can begin to influence and persuade people on different levels and with varying intensities.

Real-Life Examples of Social Pressure

You can see examples of social pressure in everyday life. From children in school, like the example we spoke about above, to football fans rioting together due to mob mentality, social pressure is everywhere. A really fantastic example of this was showcased in a television series by a hypnotist and psychological illusionist Derren Brown.

In his Apocalypse series, he was scouting for people who were susceptible enough to be hypnotized and placed through the challenges. During the vetting part of the series, he hired a room with ten chairs, in which people would come, sit down, and fill out their application form. The first two chairs had hired actors who were always there filling out the forms.

Members of the public started to walk in, sit down, and fill out their forms. Every few minutes, a bell would ding, and the two hired actors would stand until the next bell, in which they would sit back down. Members of the public were given no such instruction, but it was amazing to see that some people would stand up with the bell and the other people, but others wouldn't.

Remember, the members of the public were not given any instructions. They were simply standing up with the hired actors because social pressure told them to. They wanted to fit in and not feel as though they would be left out or were doing something wrong, perhaps because they were at fault and had missed the instructions given to them to stand.

This shows a radical change in behavior (i.e., people doing what they wouldn't normally do, simply because other people are doing it). This is reflected in all forms and cultures throughout the societies of the world, which is what makes it so powerful.

It is reflected in our societal norms, such as you need to be in a relationship to be happy. Money is a key to freedom. If you don't have lots of friends, you won't be happy. You need to be on social media. Makeup and fashion make you confident and feel good about yourself.

On a personal level, if you're in school and everyone in your class is going to college, the chances are you're going to sign up and enroll at college, too, even if it's something that you don't really want to do. To a degree, your music tastes, fashion sense, the drugs you do or don't take, and your attitude and perception you have on the world will all be dictated by the people you hang around with.

If you and your friends listen to hardcore techno music as teenagers, and you one day picked your friend up in your car while listening to Justin Bieber, you're probably going to get belittled and flamed because you're going against the social pressures set by your friend group.

There's a very fine line between doing the things you do in life because you want to do them and because it's part of the societal pressures you've been conditioned to follow, whether that's on a national basis or an individual level.

The question is, why is this social pressure so powerful?

The Science Behind Social Pressure

Social pressure is a type of influence known as "normative" influence. This is the influence where people conform to the environment they're in. Even if you're not religious and you have never been in a mosque in your life, if you were to visit one, you would take your shoes off at the door because you see everyone else is doing so. This is normative social influence at play.

This form of influence works so well because it's ingrained into your instinct, your genetics, and your millions-of-years-old brain. It's a survival tool that is the basics of what makes us humans and is responsible for how the human race got to where it is today.

Rewind back to caveman times. You're wandering around the forests or the mountains on your own. How likely are you to survive? Back then, your chances are basically zero. You'd need to do everything yourself to survive, like finding water and building camp and hunting food. If you were sick or injured, or you simply didn't have enough time to get everything done, you would die.

On the other hand, if there was a group of ten humans working together, the workload was spread out, and even if you were injured, you could be looked after until you felt better and then your chances of survival, and not just for you but for everyone in that group, is dramatically higher.

Therefore, in order for the group dynamic to work, every person in the group conforms to unwritten social standards. Everybody then feels like part of the pack and part of the group, and to differ from that image or unwritten agreement, literally as your mind is telling you, would mean death.

Nowadays, it is possible to survive on your own with very few people around you. If you had money and didn't have to work, you could live on your own and never venture outside, and you would physically survive.

I wouldn't recommend it because you'd be very lonely and would probably go crazy, but it's possible. Being a part of a group in the modern world isn't a matter of life or death, although our minds still believe it is.

Since this is the case, there's no doubt we are evolving in this new age, but these changes will take millions of years to settle in, and won't take place in our lifetime. Instead, we need to deal with the fact that conforming to social pressure is hardwired into each and every one of us.

This science of social pressure affects you in every aspect of your life. Obviously, it affects your family life and your personal relationships, but it also extends to your friend groups, offices, neighborhoods, towns, and communities. It's essential in a sense because without social pressures, the communities we live in would break down and crumble.

Social pressure has been scientifically proven over and over again, but it all started back in 1951 when social psychology researcher Solomon Asch tested this for himself. In his study, he showed people a 10 cm line labelled A on one side, and then three lines of varying sizes on the other. The three lines were 1 cm, 10 cm, and 4 cm, and labelled A, B, and C.

In the study, the lines were positioned in front of a line of ten chairs, where people sat down and were asked which line on the right-hand side was most similar to the line on the left. Of course, the answer was B. However, people were asked from left to right in the line of chairs what they thought the answer was.

Let's say you're sitting in chair seven, and you're thinking, *Of course the answer is B,* but when they start asking the people in the line, and they're answering C, you start doubting yourself. The first person answers C, and the second does, and so on, and you're left thinking, *Oh God, do they see something I don't? I don't want to be left out or the odd one out.* With this line of thinking, you cave, and despite knowing the real answer is B, you conform and state C as your answer, just like everyone else.

In this study, people were persuaded and influenced time and time again to say C, even though it's so painfully obvious the answer was B.

Harnessing the Power of Social Pressure to Persuade and Influence

As you can see from how social pressure works and how deeply ingrained it is in our being, it's an incredibly powerful tool. As someone who wants to persuade and influence people, harnessing the power of social pressure is going to be the biggest tool in your arsenal. The trick here is to trigger the social pressure response when requesting something or influencing someone, thus achieving the result you want.

Before learning how to take control of this power and learning the triggers, you need to be aware that there are two main types of social pressure, known as informative and normative influence.

We've already explored normative influence, which is by far the most powerful type of influence out of the two. In Asch's experiment, this is normative influence because people don't want to be publicly seen as being different or abnormal. In a follow-up study, people were staggered upon entry to see the lines and were told to write their answers down privately.

Of course, everyone wrote down B because their answers were private and weren't discussed with others, but as we spoke about above, people will conform when they're afraid of being rejected by others. This is known as social rejection, which is the hardwiring our brains have to help keep human beings in groups.

In comparison, informative influence occurs in situations where there is no clear goal, answer, direction, or objective. In Derren Brown's bell interview, where you would normally believe that you go into a room, sit down, and fill out an application form, a new twist has been thrown into the mix, and you're left feeling like your original belief in the matter is now no longer relevant.

You distrust your own belief to sit still and simply fill out the form when others are standing up at the sound of the bell, and instead take on the beliefs and actions of others around you, taking their beliefs and opinions as truth and making them your own. Without a word being spoken and simply through the actions of a group, you've been persuaded to change your behavior and act in a different way.

The Final Example (Darley & Latane 1968)

Okay, I've gone on and on about social pressure, so this is the last example I'm going to share. There are just so many examples of how social pressure is so powerful, and it even works in a way that can stop people from helping others, even when it's a matter of life or death. In the Darley & Latane 1968 study, they set up a simple experiment.

Participants would come into a room and talk about personal issues related to them. However, the conversations would take place over an intercom, so there was an anonymous feel to the experiment, and the participants would feel comfortable sharing information about their life. However, to help make the participants feel even more secure, the intercom would record the conversations, and the experimenters would listen to them back later.

You simply go into the room, speak into the intercom, one person at a time, and then when you're finished, you hand over the intercom to another person, and you move on, listening to the others and what they have to say from their own private room.

So, you're sitting there, and you start talking about personal issues, and one person admits that they had seizures in college, so it was a bit of a hard time for them. The conversation moves on, but suddenly out of nowhere, the person who told you they had seizures starts having one and starts pleading for help over the intercom.

What do you do?

Of course, like any sane human being, you would get up and leave the room, seeking out assistance to get medical help for the person on the other end of the intercom. In the study, when two people talked over the intercom, and the other started having a seizure, this is exactly what the participants did.

However, things changed dramatically when more people were added to the intercom discussions. When it was two people—one actor and one participant—when the actor had a seizure the participant went for help right away, but when there was more than one participant, the chances they would help dropped dramatically. The researchers actually only played the recordings of other participants, to make it seem like there were more people in the conversation, although there were still only ever two.

Turns out, when people believe there are just two people in a conversation, just them and their unknown actor, there was an 85% chance they would go for help when the actor was in danger. However, in a three-person conversation, this figure dropped to 62%, and in six people's conversations, just a measly 31%. The conclusion? People are more likely to sit and listen to someone die in group settings than get help than they would in one-to-one conversations.

How disturbing is that?

Okay, as disturbing as it may sound, there's perfectly logical explanations that again go back to how our minds work. It's all based on psychology, and by becoming aware of how it works, you can apply awareness to it in your own life, as well as taking advantage of how this psychology works.

The first psychological theory is known as diffusion of responsibility. When you're in a one-on-one situation, there are two people responsible—you and the other person. It's much easier to define who is in control and who is the authoritative person. In terms of the study, one person is healthy, and the other is having a seizure;

therefore, it's common sense that the healthy individual is the one who gets help.

On the other hand, when you have a large group of people, responsibility for any given situation is diffused, and if there's no clear leader in charge, the responsibility gets lost on individuals. This is why when people collapse in the street, people will look on, but will very rarely help. It's not their responsibility. Therefore it's not on them to act. If you're a doctor or nurse, you'll probably act because you know you're the one who needs to take action.

There are cases where people have murdered in front of people in broad daylight in the middle of the street, yet the police were only called 45 minutes later, after the victim was already dead, because out of the dozens of bystanders who witnessed the event, they all assumed (falsely) that the emergency services had already been called.

The second force is known as the audience inhibition effect, and it refers to the fact that someone may not call the police because there's a momentary glimmer that the emergency may not be real, and they don't want to risk the embarrassment of calling the emergency services in case it was a mistake, and they look stupid in front of all the people around them.

Phew! That's a lot of data. With all this information to think about when it comes to social pressure, you should start understanding how powerful this psychological force is, and it should already be clear how you can start using social pressure to influence and affect the behaviours of others. It's all about being able to exert the right amount of pressure and just the right time.

How to Apply Social Pressure When Influencing and Persuading Others

There are several ways you can apply social pressure to influence and persuade others, but you need to remember that social pressure will differ in a number of different circumstances. This includes the environment of where you are, how well everyone in the environment knows each other, how these people connect, and the social norms for the country or culture you're in.

Let's say you want to persuade someone in your office to come to the Christmas party. They don't really want to go, but you really want them to. What can you do?

One of the best ways to do this is by empathizing that attending the Christmas party is the "social norm" in your workplace. While you may not directly ask the person whether they want to come, you may talk about how exciting the idea of the party is with other people in your office who are going around them.

This will create the impression that everyone is going to the party, and everyone is looking forward to having a good time. In the mind of the person you're influencing, this is the image they'll see, thus making them feel more inclined to come. In this situation, there's also the psychological pressure of FOMO—Fear of Missing Out.

Human beings don't want to be left out of the best thing that's happened, because it makes them feel as though they've missed out on an amazing opportunity. I remember when I was in school, I had a root canal and took a week off. When I went back, I heard from all my friends that a big exciting fight happened (which is exciting when you're a kid, don't judge me) and a teacher retired, and they had a big party instead of normal lessons. This made me feel bad because I missed out, and nobody wants to feel that way.

By creating the impression that the norm in your environment is to do whatever you're trying to persuade someone to do, you're far more likely to convince that person. As I spoke about in the examples earlier in the chapter, when people are faced with group pressure, they're much more likely to conform simply because individuals don't want to be the odd one out.

Another example of a social norm you can play off is the tilt of reciprocity, or if I scratch your back, you'll scratch mine. When you do a favor for someone, this usually feels like the balance is tipped in your favor. When you've done something for someone else, more often than not, when you want a favor, they're going to be the person you go to.

This is another form of social pressure that you can take advantage of. This works very well and is a very powerful method of persuasion because not following through on the favor dramatically increases the risk of social rejection, therefore being an outcast in the group.

For example, Bill and Andy are neighbors. Bill breaks his leg and is recovering at home, even though he has some jobs in the garden to do. He's talking with Andy over the fence one day, and Andy goes, "Don't worry, Bill. Your grass is growing long, but I'll cut it as a favor." Andy cuts the lawn, and Bill is happy with his garden.

Now, when Andy has something that he wants done, the chances that Bill is going to accept the favor are very high. If Bill says no to the favor, or any subsequent favors until the scales of reciprocity are balanced, how's that going to make Bill look in front of the neighborhood?

Andy will tell everyone how selfish Bill is, and when Bill really needed help, Andy was there to help, but when it was the other way around, Bill just made excuses and did his own thing. This is going to make Bill look very bad and will turn the neighborhood against him. He obviously doesn't want this, so conforms to Andy's favor, regardless of whether or not he wants to do it.

Now, it's worth noting that usually the scales will need to be balanced with equal parts. So if Andy cuts Bill's lawn, Andy is then owed a favor of an equal caliber, such as help in the garden that takes the same amount of time, a lift to the airport, or something along these lines. However, if you can build up favors with someone to a point where they owe you a lot, then you may be able to ask for even bigger favors.

People tend to be forgetful when it comes to things like this, so make it very clear, but remain friendly with what you've done for people. A gentle reminder can be enough for the other person to think. *Okay, yeah, you have helped me a lot. I can now help you.*

As you can see, playing off social norms plays a big part in adding pressure. I've spoken a little bit about mob mentality, and this is an extreme version of social pressure. Imagine you have a football stadium, and the home team loses. Everyone, angry and upset with the result, walks out onto the street after the game, and tensions are high.

One person reacts by kicking over a bin or throwing something at the fans of the other team, and suddenly the crowd erupts. Because one person has thrown something, suddenly, this justifies the actions of everyone doing it. If one person has done it and got away with it, then why can't everyone else?

Of course, specifically with mob mentality, there's a degree of anonymity, so people believe they won't be caught and penalized for their actions because they're unrecognizable in a crowd of people, but you can see what I mean when I say that even in an intense situation like a football stadium car park, when the norm of that environment changes, people are very quick to attach to these ideas and change their behaviors and what they deem acceptable and normal very quickly.

This leads us very nicely into our next chapter, where we're going to be talking about creating even more "normal" situations in which the traditional norms of environments can be changed to suit the outcome you're trying to achieve.

Chapter Eight – How Repetition Changes Everything

"It's the repetition of affirmations that leads to belief. And once that belief becomes a deep conviction, things begin to happen." – Muhammad Ali

Playing off the last chapter, you should start to see how interesting social norms are. When you travel from the Western world to the Eastern world, you may see scenes that shock you. When I first traveled to India in my twenties, I saw naked women washing clothes in the streets, and children running around the road while men butchered and skinned cattle next to the dusty paths. At first, I was in shock with how all these things were happening so openly, but I soon realized that this is just the norm in other countries. Most countries, societies, and nations are unique in their own way.

This happens everywhere in the world, on both big and small scales. Some families are very strict, disciplined, and will sit down and have dinner with each member of the family present every single night. Some families don't eat together, but instead eat whenever they want, usually in front of the television. Some families will dress up nicely every day, and some families are nudists.

This is again reflected in the business world. Some companies are known for being professionally styled businesses where everyone needs to wear a suit and must present themselves in a smart fashion, and in other companies, employees are allowed to wear whatever they want, be it jeans and a hoodie or otherwise.

Norms change all the time, depending on what we're used to and subject too.

So, bearing this in mind and pulling it back to taking control of this psychology, when it comes to influencing people, a powerful way to do so, thus changing and influencing someone's behavior, is to make your message consistent, normal, and habitual.

Meet Mark. Hi, Mark. Mark works for a software company and wears a suit to the office. He plays golf on the weekends and goes to bars with friends. He's not very cultured but likes to live for the weekend. One night in his favorite bar, he meets Melissa. Mark thinks Melissa is a "bit hippie," since she wears colorful dresses and scarves, and isn't really his type.

She likes yoga and spending her weekends in museums and art galleries. While very different, they hit it off and swap phone numbers and go on several dates. They get on well, and one day, Melissa invites Mark to join her at a yoga class. Now, ask Mark that question months ago, he would have said "absolutely not," and still does.

Melissa talks about the benefits of going and what she likes about it. It does her good and makes her feel good. When she gets in from her yoga class, she talks about how much better she feels and how the people there are always so nice. Over time, and by consistently sending a positive message, Mark agrees to join Melissa for a class, and he loves it. Now Mark loves yoga.

This is a very common example of how people can change their attitudes, beliefs, and behaviors when a message is made normal and is habitually sent. Mark would never have been around anybody who even spoke about yoga in the office and would have just a brief understanding of what it would have been like from the advertisements and shows he sees on TV.

However, over time, Melissa sends messages that make the practice of yoga become normal in Mark's life until it gets to a point where his behavior and attitude finally changes. In this example, this happens very naturally and probably without Melissa doing anything, so now imagine what you'll be able to achieve if you're consciously implementing this technique in your interactions.

So, how do you do it?

Implement Repetitive Messages

When you want to form a new habit in your life, like running or eating properly, how do you do it? Well, you start doing it, and you try to be as consistent as you can. You do that thing over and over again, repeating it over and over until it finally becomes a normal part of your daily routine, and therefore a generated and nurtured habit. This mentality needs to be applied to the message you're sending.

Whether you're a lover or a hater of Donald Trump, there's no denying that his message stating "Make America Great Again" is an incredibly powerful form of persuasion. The message was repeated everywhere, across all his branding, television shows, hats, online content, banners, and more. It's this repetition that fixates in the minds of America that drives his campaign forward.

The brain loves to be comfortable. As a survival tool, if the brain recognizes something repeatedly, and it knows it to be a safe situation, then it's happy, and it will make you feel happy because your brain wants you to be safe. If you're put in a room with twelve scary looking bodyguards, you'll feel on edge. However, if you're familiar with these bodyguards, say they're your friends, you'll feel completely at ease.

This is known as the mere exposure effect, or the familiarity principle, a term coined by Robert Zajonc.

When you're subject to something repeatedly, you begin to develop a positive mindset towards it as it becomes your comfort zone. This is why people go to bars and order the same drinks, the same item off the menu of their favorite restaurant, or become attached to the people in their lives.

There are plenty of examples where science has proven this to be the case. Researchers Mita, Dermer, and Knight, 1977, carried out a survey where they showed people and their friends two pictures: one of a person and one of their reflected selves. The results showed that individuals much preferred the photo of their reflected selves, whereas their friends preferred the actual unreflected photo of themselves.

When you consider that most of us walk around the house all day and only ever see the reflected version of ourselves, it's easy to see why the outcome was this. If you take a photo of yourself on your phone and then flip it using the editing features (available in the Photos app on most smartphones), you'll see what you'll actually look like to others, and it's probably going to make you feel really uncomfortable because you're not used to it. On the other hand, if you saw this image of yourself every day, you'd become used to it and even happy with it. This is the power of the repeated message.

The science behind this is also very simple. Imagine your mind is a jungle, and every time you do something, anything, a little version of you makes it way through the jungle. For example, you're learning how to play tennis. Every time you play, the little mental version of you is cutting through the jungle from one side to the other. This path represents the neural pathways in your brain. The more you practice tennis, the stronger these pathways become and the easier and more fluent at the task you become.

In the jungle metaphor, this is like starting something new for the first time, and you have to cut your way through the neural jungle with a machete. There are thick vines and undergrowth in your way. However, the more you walk that path, over time, it starts to clear. A small track is formed, and that turns into a big open tunnel through the jungle.

Over the years, you lay a concrete path through that jungle until eventually, you end up with a twelve-lane superhighway where you can travel down that same path at super speed. That's when you become incredibly familiar with doing something, which can only ever be achieved through repetition.

Now relate this concept to how you send your message to others.

In the beginning, if you're proposing something completely new and radical, people are going to take this message and, in their minds, it will be like cutting through the thick jungle of the brain. However, through repetition, you can start to clear the trees and undergrowth until a clear path is formed and the message becomes their norm.

There are several ways you can do this when it comes to persuading and influencing people.

How to Influence and Persuade People Through Repetition

Through the rest of this chapter, I'm going to talk you through the process of introducing a concept to someone and then making that message habitual enough through repetition that it becomes their norm.

Make the Message Simple

First things first, you need to send your message in the clearest and easiest way you possibly can. This is a process known as conceptual fluency. It states that the faster you can comprehend information coming into your brain, the higher the chance is that you will have a positive relationship with it.

If you've never played a game of chess and I tell you a Ka3+ would have been a great move to counter their Rb4, you'll have no idea what I'm talking about, and you'll probably be rather put off by the information. You mentally shove it away from you and want nothing to do with it. This is because you won't understand the complex chess language, and the idea feels too complicated.

Of course, through repetition and positive reinforcement, this could change over time, but you can't lead with that. Instead, if I said, "You can move your knight diagonally on a chessboard," this information is very easy to understand, and you'll be much more likely to have a positive relationship with it.

Think about this from a business perspective. If I said go out and buy some new trainers to start running with, you're probably going to buy from the brand you know the most because this is what is familiar to you and you understand it. There's no learning process that needs to take place. This is why marketing companies spend billions every year trying to make their brand the most recognizable to you in the simplest way possible.

Let's look at a real-life example.

You're trying to persuade your friend to come and see a new movie with you. This movie is not really your friend's taste, and they're indifferent to the idea, but you really want someone to go with you, and it would be nice to spend some time with them. How do you approach it?

Instead of going straight in by asking them to see the movie with you, talk about going to the movies with them, but not about anything specifically. Say things like

"Ah, we haven't been to the cinema in such a long time. We should think about going," or "When was the last time you went to the cinema and saw something good?" You may want to be more specific, saying something like, "I love the sound quality of a cinema viewing. There's just no experience like it. It's the best way to enjoy movies."

When you do this for a couple of days, you're priming your friend with positive repetition. After a few days, your friend will have a positive mindset towards going to the cinema, in which they're much more likely to say yes to your request. It's all about building them up first before diving into requesting something from someone.

Use Repetitions in Every Possible Sense

You can get creative with the way you repeat something to someone, and the more creative you can be, and the more ways you can repeat something, the more you're going to drive home your message. When it comes to writing a book like this, the layout is always the same in every chapter. I use the same fonts and the same size headers and chapter indicators.

Every chapter is laid out in the same way and written in the same format. This is a form of repetition. Imagine if each chapter was written differently with a different font. You'd be uncomfortable and have no idea what's going on and why, and you wouldn't end up reading the book, let alone absorbing the message that's being shared.

The human brain loves consistency and repetition, so do it in every possible way. If you're asking your colleague to the Christmas party as we spoke about in the last chapter, always ask in the same way. This means asking the same question and talking in the same volume and using the same tone of voice.

Really imagine if something asked you something three times in three different ways. The first time they whispered it to you, and the next, they shouted. Not only would you think they're crazy, but you're also definitely not going to agree with what they're saying.

Chapter Nine – Incentivise!
Rewarding for Results

"An incentive is a bullet, a key: An often tiny object with astonishing power to change a situation." – Steven Levitt

The title of this chapter says it all and really needs no introduction. If you want your kid to behave while shopping in the grocery store, you promise them sweets in return for good behavior. You get what you want on the promise that the other party will get something in return. It happens with dogs very clearly. You want them to behave or learn a new trick, you give them treats. It's an exchange that takes place, and it works exceptionally well within human beings.

The thing is, offering a dog or a child a reward for good behavior seems and feels like pretty standard stuff, but how far could you take it? How could you incentivize others as a means of persuading them to do something, and does it actually work similarly to the other ways we've already spoken about in this book?

Is there science and principle behind the concept?

Back in 1938, B.F Skinner, one of the best-known behavioral psychologists in the world, decided to find out. He ran an experiment that gave pigeons treats at set times. While completely unrelated to the pigeon's behaviors, the birds started to mimic the exact behavior they did before the treat was dispensed. For example, if a pigeon bobbed their head or made a sound and a treat came out, they would then repeat this action in the hopes of receiving more food.

In the experiment, one bird made a habit of turning counterclockwise, two or three turns between receiving a treat.

This may sound simple at best, and humans are, of course, very different from pigeons, but then again, are we really? How many people do you know who have a ritual or a "lucky thing" they do before they do something major? Many motivational speakers of the world jump on trampolines or physically move around to get their heart rates up before going out on stage to boost their energy levels. Yes, they can bring more energy into the event on a physical level, but it's really a behavioral ritual that gets the motivational speaker into a performing mindset.

Let's say that every time you got into the car, you touched wood as a good luck sign that nothing bad was going to happen. You get in the car, drive to work, and everything's fine. You do this again and again, and before you know it, touching wood is something you need to do every time you get in a car. Some people will actually be fearful something bad is going to happen if they break this ritual.

This is a prime example of incentivizing to modify your behavior. You do something, and something good comes from it. You know what I'm talking about, so I don't think there's any need to go much further into it, but in line with the purpose of this book, how can you utilize this as a behavioral strategy?

Let's find out.

A Persuasion Strategy Through Incentives

Right off the bat, you need to understand that providing any kind of incentive isn't going to just work and persuade people to do things for you, change their behavior, nor make them act a certain way. For example, I'll give you a bag of sweets if you tidy my entire house top to bottom, dust everything, and do a really professional job.

The incentive isn't enough for the action, highlighting the two variables you need to be thinking about: A) what you're using as an incentive and B) what the behavioral change or action is. This leads us to the two types of motivation you need to be thinking about.

Intrinsic Motivation and Extrinsic Motivation.

Intrinsic motivation is a motivation that comes from the heart and is something that someone is personally interested in. For example, there could be a task that someone finds enjoyable, so they're happy to do it. This is intrinsic. This could mean going clothes shopping, ordering food, or writing a book. People are intrinsically doing something because it brings them personal value.

On the other hand, extrinsic value is all about getting something external. You may ask someone to help you move to a new house. They don't necessarily want to do it, and it's not a truly enjoyable task, but you promised them pizza and beer afterward, so that makes it worthwhile. Of course, some actions can be both intrinsic and extrinsic, but here's where you can start persuading people.

First, understand that intrinsic motivation is almost always the main approach to influence you're going to want to focus on because it's far more effective. It's like asking what you would do for a million dollars. Everything has a limit, and some people would do some stuff for free, and some people would need more than a million dollars. This is the power of intrinsic motivation.

So, let's get into the meat of this.

Defining the Quantity of the Incentive

In the situation where you're persuading someone, size really does matter. When you ask a favor from someone, you may think that giving them $10,000 is a great incentive, for example. Most people would think that's a great incentive, especially in comparison to a $1,000 incentive. After all, you're getting ten times more as a reward.

While this may seem like the case in your head, it can actually have the opposite effect in reality. When the incentive is too big, this can cause people to feel pressured to perform, and it can put people off going through with whatever they've agreed to do. A chess lover could go to a tournament with a $100 prize and do really well. The $100 is great if they win, but not too problematic if they lose. Alternatively, a $100,000 prize fund is a lot of money, a lot of pressure, which can put people off.

So, big incentives are bad and small incentives are good? Not entirely. It's a little more complicated than that. It's about finding the balance per situation, but it's also so much more than that. Back in 2009, Uri Gneezy conducted an experiment where students were told to go and collect money as donations.

There were three groups of students who went out. The first would receive 10% of the donations they made. The second would receive 1%, and the last would receive nothing. They would collect the donations, and all the money would go elsewhere. Who do you think made the most?

Common sense would suggest that students receiving the 10% donations would make the most because they would have the largest incentive to make more, but the reality turned out to be quite different. The student group who made nothing on the donations actually made the most, but why? Science shows, in particular Harmon-Jones, 2000, that when people are seeking rewards, they tend not to focus on the task at hand but are more focused on what they are getting out of it.

In this example, the people who were making 10% were focused on making as much money as possible, maybe even seeming desperate, because they wanted to make the most. The group earning 0% was only focused on collecting donations for the causes. This means less pressure on the money collecting aspect, and a more relaxed approach, thus generating more donations.

This relates back to intrinsic and extrinsic. If the incentive is too big, then it may become more extrinsic. This can work in some cases, but for long-term behavioral change, an intrinsic incentive is always going to be better. If the person you're persuading thinks that they're doing something because it will benefit them in the long term, this is a much more effective way of sending your message.

118

For example, if you're an employer and trying to make your staff work harder, you could do two things—pay them more, or offer incentives to move up the ranks into your management team. You could say, "If we hit targets this year, then everyone gets a bonus." This works in many amazing ways, and people will tend to work harder to hit targets, but this remains extrinsic. Once targets have been hit and the bonus paid out, you'll need to offer another bonus next year to achieve the same results.

On a more individual level, however, if you were to offer someone the chance to progress up the ranks of your company, you could do so by claiming that they'll earn more money long term and will have authority within your business, and it will look good on their resume, opening a whole new range of opportunities for them in their future.

This idea of a promotion then appeals to the intrinsic nature of the employee, because they'll be working hard to benefit themselves and grow themselves, as well as benefiting the business. When it comes to work targets, this person working their way up is much more likely to strive to hit targets year after year after year. See the difference?

What can you learn from all this?

Sometimes, incentives can be big. If you want someone to do something for you as a one-off, then the bigger your incentive is, the better. However, if you want long-lasting behavioral changes, a smaller, more intrinsic incentive could be the better option.

Define What the Incentive Is

Of course, you need to think about what you're giving someone as an incentive. I've already spoken a lot about money and financial incentive being a great way to influence someone, but it's not always possible nor suitable to use money. This could be seen as bribing, and that's not a great way to be seen.

Take a look at this list of incentives you could use and try and see what kind of scope you can develop in your mind:

- Buying someone takeout
- Offering to take someone out
- Buying someone flowers
- Giving someone a hug
- Giving someone the opportunity to explore their creative passions
- Having the experience of a lifetime
- Praise and positive feedback
- Recognition
- Status

- A position of power

This is just a handful of ways you can incentivize people. A lot of people won't need money or anything physical but would rather be recognized for the work they do. Remember the story I was telling you a few chapters back when I worked in a supermarket under two team leaders? The female team leader was so talkative when it came to singing praises for the work that people had done.

I remember one Christmas, the store had a huge delivery, and we knew the work list wasn't going to be completed by the end of our shift when it should have been. However, the team leader motivated us to work hard, stating how we were all in this together, and everything was going well.

When I had finished my first job, I remembered her coming up to me and saying something along the lines of, "Well done, it's really appreciated how hard you worked to get that done. Thank you." Her words warmed something inside of me, and although I knew I only worked at a supermarket and was stacking shelves, I felt immense pride for the work I had done. I was recognized and appreciated. I was a valued member of the team.

Incentives can come in the form of anything; it's simply about tapping into the most intrinsic form of motivation you can think of in any situation. This will vary from person to person and will depend on the relationship you develop with them. If you need a recap, flick back to chapter four on nurturing a good relationship with people.

The more you know about another person and understand them, the more accurately you'll be able to incentivize them using intrinsic motivation. In some cases, you may even be able to give people their own choice, literally enabling them to tell you what incentive they would like. In some businesses, you may ask whether someone wants lieu days in payment for their overtime shifts or flat-out payment.

This can actually be a much more satisfying approach for the other person because they feel in control and as though you're giving something they want, something they are choosing to have. In reality, this is a false sense of control because you're clearly willing to incentivize with either to persuade them to do what it is you want them to do.

There's no denying that incentivizing someone when persuading or attempting to influence them is one of the most tried-and-tested approaches that deliver consistent results. When all else fails, you can pretty much guarantee that this is an approach that can work, but it's all about getting creative.

If you're a manager of a company and you're looking to fill overtime shifts desperately, you could ask and hope for the best, you could offer time and a half, or you could simply approach the situation in a way that makes the person want to work for you for nothing. This can only be achieved from positive interactions, a consideration that applies to every single persuasion method I've spoken about already.

This is the power of positivity.

Chapter Ten – The Power of Positivity

"Once you replace negative thoughts with positive ones, you'll start having positive results."

– Willie Nelson

When I raised my idea for writing this book with my friends and family, some aired some concerns I hadn't thought about.

"Is it possible to persuade someone to take drugs, or commit a crime?"

"Could you manipulate someone into sleeping with you or going on a date? That's illegal. That's blackmail. That's immoral."

I thought about this for some time. While I like to look at the world positively and optimistically, there's no denying that there are people out there who are manipulative and immoral. Some people use the techniques in this book for their own personal gain and wish to harm others. I am not advocating this in any way, but it's an important topic to touch upon.

I've tried to write this chapter about a dozen times now, and I've never been sure how to approach it until I was sitting in a cafe one Saturday afternoon watching the world go by, and I saw a mother talking with her child. The kid must have been no older than four or five, and he was captivated by the dog laying on the floor, sleeping at the feet of his owner at another table. The mother was talking with a friend, and the kid kept walking over, smiling at the owner and then eagerly waiting to stroke the dog. The dog opened an eye and shut it again, indifference to the child's presence.

I watched for several minutes as the mother called her child back, told him to sit down next to her, and then carried on her conversation. The child would wait, never once taking his eyes off the dog, and would slowly get up and make his way back over. This happened three or four times before the mother snapped. Everyone jumped and looked in her direction, including the dog who had now sat bolt upright and stared with those absolute black eyes.

"GET OVER HERE THIS INSTANT AND DO NOT MOVE A MUSCLE AGAIN."

Her voice was terrifying. If I were the four-year-old, I probably would have cried my eyes out. Poor kid is probably going to have some kind of later life trauma related to his childhood. He didn't cry. He just solemnly walked back to the seat and sat. All the spark of happiness had gone from his eyes, and I couldn't help but feel bad for him. This was obviously something the kid had gone through before. You could see it in his face.

And then it hit me.

As human beings, we always have a choice on how we act and address certain situations. In this story, the mother lost her rag and went full-blown nuclear in a matter of minutes because she didn't have the time or patience to explain to the child what she wanted to do. Her persuasion and interpersonal skills were clearly non-existent, and I'm not to judge another's parenting skills, but I would do things so differently.

Sure, kids can be annoying at times, but it was clear that this explosive and ballistic approach doesn't work. It never does. Sure enough, a few minutes later, the color had returned to the kid's face, and he was back on the cafe floor, making his way over to the dog. The mother looked over, muttered something under her breath, and gave up.

While being forceful and aggressive with people can seem like a surefire way to make things happen, feeding off the fear of others and basically forcing them into a corner, this doesn't come without consequence and it doesn't ever have a lasting effect.

Imagine you're in a board meeting, and you're pitching an idea. There are two ideas, and the votes are evenly split. One person is left to vote, so you grab him by the cuff of the neck, throw him against a wall, and demand he votes for your idea, or else. He may well indeed vote for your idea out of fear, but your reputation is ruined, and people are never going to look at you the same way.

On the other hand, taking this guy to dinner and talking over your idea in a bit more detail, giving him some insight and giving him your full, undivided attention to make him feel like the center of your universe is a much more effective approach that is going to deliver much better results both short and long term.

Long story short, positivity works, and here's how.

Positive Interactions Deliver Positive Results

Think about the last chapter and how if I asked you to help me move to a new house, I would treat you to pizza and beer at the end of the day. This is a very positive experience because I've created the image that we're going to work hard together in moving all my stuff, and then we can sit back and relax and enjoy the fruits of our labor with some good food and drink. It's a positive image that makes you want to be involved.

This positive reinforcement in my message (which in this case is asking you to help me move to a new house) starts from the moment I start talking about moving to a new house. If I was to say, "Oh, I have to move because I've been kicked out of my apartment. I've broken up with my partner, and I'm so sad."

This creates a very negative association with the idea of moving to a new house right off the bat. Then when it comes to your request, the other person is going to want to be as far as possible from this negative experience and will probably do all they can to get out of it, whether that's making excuses or flat out saying no.

Take the same people in the same situation, but instead, I say, "I'm moving to a new house next week. It's been a rough few weeks, having broken up with my girlfriend, but I'm ready to start moving forward and begin the next chapter of my life. I just need some help moving some stuff, and I'm all set to go."

This is the exact same request in the exact same circumstances, but the positive spin reframes the message in an entirely new way. It's far more positive, and far more likely, the person will want to be involved. When you add the incentive of pizza and beer afterward, the offer becomes a no-brainer.

Whenever you're heading into a situation when you're persuading or influencing someone, always craft and frame your message in the most positive way possible. That doesn't mean you need to lie and make everything seem like all sunshine and rainbows when it isn't but add a positive spin.

Note any animal welfare charity advertisements you may see on TV. They always show animals in heart-wrenching conditions that can make you squirm in your seat. The pain in their eyes. The horrible conditions. The blood or tattered fur. It's horrible to watch, and the very essence of a negative message, but the ads don't stop there.

They always move on, saying how you can help, and how your money can help turn this rescue dog into this, and then they show the same dog but a much happier and healthier version which is about to be rehomed to a loving family, and it's a very heartwarming story.

This is how effective you can be at reframing a negative message and turning it into something positive. It doesn't matter what message you're sending, whether it's inherently positive or negative, you can always make it positive with the right spin. There are plenty of ways you can do this, including:

- Reframing your message with a positive attitude
- Using positive language
- Create a positive situation when discussing the matter
- Using positive reinforcement
- Using positive associations

Now, there are variations on this, and the subject of being "positive" is not so black and white. For example, if you're trying to persuade a group of people to vote for a certain political party, you may not want to be positive in the traditional sense, but you may want to get people angry.

You could do this by highlighting all the negatives that are currently a problem in the current government, and then detail how your political party will make positive changes. You could rile up your audience to get them angry at the current government. You could make them livid and want to protest and riot (although I'm not recommending this at all). The point is that at the foundation of everything, the message you're sending is that you want positive change, and you're encouraging others to see your view in the same way.

Let's look into some more practical persuasion strategies along this line.

Turning Negative Message Positive Through Slow Repetition

Let's say that you have a child who refuses to brush their teeth at night. They hate it, and it's always a hassle trying to get them into the bathroom to the sink, and it's a fuss and stress you don't want to deal with anymore. What do you do?

Well, you could shout at your kid and force them to get on with it, or you could change what is already associated as being a negative experience as being a positive one. You can do this by slowly changing the situation a little bit at a time. Another common example of this, again children-related, is getting them to eat vegetables at dinner they don't want to eat.

You start at the beginning. When it's time for your kid to brush their teeth, you start with positive language. If it's a problem so far, then you've probably shown your kid through your body language and verbal language that it's a stressful time, and problems are to be expected, so don't bring that back into the situation. Instead, remain fun, positive, and engaging.

This will certainly surprise your child, but they're probably still going to resist. No matter. If you keep implementing this positivity night after night without fail, a little bit at a time, slowly but surely, your kid will start to get used to it and will start seeing the time to brush their teeth as a positive time. This is a process known as **systematic desensitization**.

You can apply this in any situation. Say you're at work, and everyone goes into the morning meeting but always sighs and groans when it's time to go in, so you decide to switch things up and make a change. You become more engaging, and you make your body language and verbal language more charismatic and confident.

People in the meeting enjoy this new meeting, but they will still mumble and groan because it's probably a one-off. However, over time you keep implementing this energy into your meetings, and slowly the mentality of people starts to change. A once-negative experience becomes positive. Once people have had a positive experience for long enough, they'll suddenly notice that what they once hated they now love, and because they love it, they're going to keep doing it.

The moral of this story: Work hard at desensitizing any negative messages by turning them positive. Be patient and watch the results unfold before your very eyes.

Persuading Through Repeated Positive Exposure

Let's say it's getting close to the yearly family vacation and you're looking for somewhere to go. The wife wants to go to Paris because it's romantic and beautiful, and it's always near the top of her bucket list. Her husband wants to do a road trip across Germany because he saw a car documentary and thought the route would be something he'd love to see from himself. Already we find ourselves at a bit of a stalemate.

What can the wife do to persuade her husband?

In this case, positive repeated exposure would be a great way to go forward. The husband may have his own thoughts about Paris. Maybe he thinks it's too full of tourists, or there's nothing that will take his fancy, so even without going, he's already created this idea in his head that he doesn't want to go. A negative situation, in this case, a negative thought against going to Paris. He's already created this thought association through repetition. Now it's up to his wife to reverse the thinking.

By subtly watching shows featuring Paris that will appeal to her husband's interest, leaving open websites on the shared computer, dropping in Paris in positive conversations, and maybe not so subtly leaving travel guides open about Paris, suddenly her husband starts to see Paris everywhere. As long as it's in a positive light, he'll start developing positive associations with the city.

Over time, just like the child brushing his teeth, lots of little positive reinforcements will slowly change his mind to see the subject in a positive light. When that next "where do you want to go on vacation" conversation comes around again, he's in a much more likely position to say yes.

When you think about it, it goes without saying that the more positively we think about something, the more we're going to resonate with it, but you can have more control over what people think is positive just through subtle cues and repetitions.

As you've probably guessed from reading chapter to chapter, the best way to persuade and influence people is by combining a lot of the various methods and meshing them all together. For example, you may want to incentivize someone, but you're going to borrow elements of positive persuasion to make it work.

With the kid brushing his teeth (last time I'm mentioning this kid, I swear), if he can brush his teeth and have a positive experience, with the incentive of having a bedtime story afterward, he's far more likely to brush his teeth without any hassle.

Of course, how you approach a certain situation, a certain person or group of people can vary dramatically depending on the individual circumstances you're in, which you're only going to figure out with practice and mastering these methods over time. This is exactly what we're going to focus on in our final chapter.

Chapter Eleven – Getting Better with Practice (Tips & Tricks)

"Knowledge is of no value unless you put it into practice." – Anton Chekhov

As you near the end of your journey into mastering the art of persuasion and influence, an art that has never been more important in a world where communication is everything, sending a powerful and direct message has become harder than ever. There's just one more point you need to look at, bringing everything you've learned together.

Throughout this book's chapters, we've dived into all kinds of persuasion methods and approaches, from reading someone's body language to using NLP and more. It's a lot of information there to process, and you're probably left wondering, *How the hell am I supposed to bring all of this together?*

For starters, you've probably noticed that I keep referring to this process as "the art of persuasion." You may have just overlooked that as fancy wording, or you might see some truth to it, but it's crucial to your success that you start seeing your acts of influence and persuasion as indeed an art form.

Why?

What is art?

It's the ability to share strong emotions. It challenges the beliefs of the mind and expands understanding. It's complicated at times, and you can be sharing both simple and complex methods simultaneously. It's about sending a message and sharing a point of view, usually an original idea, and all of these factors are present in all forms of art.

From songs and paintings to drawings and books, persuasion is, at its very core, a form of art. It's part of the art of communication. And, just like an artist of any medium, you need to practice getting better. Nobody, or very rarely, can someone pick up a paintbrush and create a magnificent work of art that's adored by millions.

You need to pick up the paintbrush and try it out for yourself. You then need to explore how different brushstrokes work on various canvases and materials. You need to experiment with different colors and blend them to see what happens. You then need to fine-tune your technique and inventory by using better paintbrushes and upgrading the tools you use once you're ready to move on and know what you're doing.

James W. Williams

This is exactly what you need to be doing when it comes to mastering the art of persuasion.

Using the information in this book, you'll need to figure out what works for you and each individual situation you're in. This can admittedly feel overwhelming at times, but with time and practice, you'll get better and better until it becomes second nature. You've just got to take those first steps and try.

It doesn't matter what walk of life you're from. Whether you're using persuasion in an obvious sense, perhaps if you're in business and working with clients, or in sales and communicating with customers, or you're trying to teach your kids new and healthy habits and life skills, or convincing your partner to go on a road trip you've always wanted to go on, persuasion is not manipulative or evil. It's merely a term used to describe the process of better communication.

It's interesting because now that you know and understand the factors that go into the art of persuasion, you'll start seeing people who do it to you, conversations and approaches you may never have noticed before. Many people do things unconsciously, such as using certain kinds of body language, but you'll soon be able to tell who's been practicing for themselves, and this a great way to learn for yourself.

Okay, okay, so how do you practice this fine art?

137

First, you're going to want to start small.

You can start with whatever you want and feel comfortable with, but I recommend starting with body language. This is where I started, and it was incredibly helpful when it came to mastering my body language and reading it in other people. You can then move onto more complex approaches, such as priming and finding incentives.

You can practice aspects of persuasion, like bringing a more positive tone into your language, at any time. Try writing or speaking and recording what you say and then listening to it back and seeing how you can make things better. The key is to be conscious and aware of your interactions with other people. Many people simply go through their lives unconsciously, just repeating their old habits and reactionary patterns and never expanding their horizons nor trying anything new. Once you understand this and can bring awareness to this, you start to grow and nurture real change in many areas throughout your life.

For the most part, much of your learning experience will come with trial and error, figuring out what works and what doesn't. You'll start seeing what works and what doesn't, what you feel comfortable with, and what techniques you enjoy using. This, like with any other skill a human being can learn these days, will help you get better and more skilled over time.

You'll also need to make sure you're focusing on the core foundations of what it means to influence and persuade someone. This means focusing on building a connection—a genuine connection—with the people you're speaking too. You're creating a relationship based on trust and honesty because nobody will be persuaded by someone who is neither of these things.

And so, with all this in mind and to summarize everything we've spoken about and to help you move forward in this new journey, here's the lowdown on this book, and the core points you're going to want to remember:

- Nurture trust
- Create a genuine connection
- Focus on powerful and effective communication
- Be positive
- Listen and understand the other person
- Mirror the other person
- Always appeal to wants over needs
- Be confident and assured in yourself
- Be focused and present in your interactions and conversations
- Practice at every opportunity

If you can bear these core points in mind, and then couple these with the techniques, approaches, and persuasive methods you've learned through this book, you'll be a master persuader in no time at all. Now it's over to you.

Chapter Twelve – Final Thoughts

And we have officially reached the end of your journey into the art of persuasion. How do you feel? Have you already tried using some of these techniques in your own life, or are you getting ready to start practicing them? It can be a very exciting time when you start using them for the first time, and then after a short time, you'll start to see fantastic results.

You'll also see these techniques come in handy in other parts of your life. The chapter on being able to read people's body language brought so many benefits into my life, especially into my romantic relationships where I was able to better understand the people I love and see what they were trying to say to me, as well as being able to communicate more effectively. It's a lot of fun and bringing it all together, there's no doubt in my mind you're about to embark on a new chapter of your life in a direction you've never seen before!

Good luck!

Speaking of new directions, if you enjoyed this book, it would be gratefully appreciated if you could leave a positive review detailing what you thought. Writing books like this has been such an amazing journey for me, and I adore the amount of value that can be shared through texts just like this one. I hear so many stories of people who use their takeaways to change their lives, and I want to hear yours! Practice the methods, give it some time, see the results, and then I'd love to hear your thoughts!

Lastly, don't forget to grab a copy of your Free Bonus book *Bulletproof Confidence Checklist*. If you want to learn how to overcome shyness and social anxiety and become more confident, then this book is for you.

Just go to: https://theartofmastery.com/confidence/

It takes a lot of time to write a book like this, and as you can see from some of the chapters, it can get very personal in places, but that's because human communication is such a personal thing, and until we start perceiving it like that, we'll find ourselves stuck in the same old loops, relationships, jobs, and situations we've always found ourselves in.

It's time to start living the life you want to live, so buckle up and get going!

References

Kibler, J. (1970, January 01). Cognitive Schemas. Retrieved October 05, 2020, from https://link.springer.com/referenceworkentry/10.1007/978-0-387-79061-9_608

Segaert, Katrien. (2018). Priming Effects. 10.1007/978-3-319-28099-8_479-1.

Bargh, J. A., Chen, M., & Burrows, L. (1996). Automaticity of social behavior: Direct effects of trait construct and stereotype activation on action. *Journal of Personality and Social Psychology, 71*(2), 230-244. doi:10.1037/0022-3514.71.2.230

Hagood EW, Gruenewald TL. Positive versus negative priming of older adults' generative value: do negative messages impair memory? *Aging Ment Health.* 2018;22(2):257-260. doi:10.1080/13607863.2016.1239063

Neuroskeptic. (2019, November 19). Words On The Brain: A Semantic Map of the Cortex. Retrieved October 05, 2020, from https://www.discovermagazine.com/mind/words-on-the-brain-a-semantic-map-of-the-cortex

Collins, A. M., & Loftus, E. F. (1975). A spreading-activation theory of semantic processing.

Psychological Review, 82, 407-428. http://dx.doi.org/10.1037/0033-295X.82.6.407

Neuro-linguistic programming (NLP): Does it work? (n.d.). Retrieved October 05, 2020, from https://www.medicalnewstoday.com/articles/320368

Thompson, J. (2011, September 30). Is Nonverbal Communication a Numbers Game? Retrieved October 05, 2020, from https://www.psychologytoday.com/us/blog/beyond-words/201109/is-nonverbal-communication-numbers-game

Thompson, J. (2012, February 20). Embodied Cognition: What It Is & Why It's Important. Retrieved October 05, 2020, from https://www.psychologytoday.com/us/blog/beyond-words/201202/embodied-cognition-what-it-is-why-its-important

Wagenmakers, E. & Beek, Titia & Dijkhoff, Laura & Gronau, Quentin & Acosta, Alberto & Jr, Adams, & Albohn, Daniel & Allard, Eric & Benning, Stephen & Blouin-Hudon, Eve-Marie & Bulnes, Luis Carlo & Caldwell, Tracy & Calin-Jageman, Robert & Capaldi, Colin & Carfagno, Nicholas & Chasten, Kelsie & Cleeremans, Axel & Connell, Louise & DeCicco, Jennifer & Zwaan, Rolf. (2016). Registered Replication Report: Strack, Martin, &

Stepper (1988). Perspectives on Psychological Science. 11. 917-928. 10.1177/1745691616674458.

Asch, S. E. (1956). Asch Conformity Task. *PsycTESTS Dataset*. doi:10.1037/t31951-000

Darley, J. M., & Latané, B. (1968). Bystander intervention in emergencies: Diffusion of responsibility. Journal of Personality and Social Psychology, 8, 377-383.

Mita, T. H., Dermer, M., & Knight, J. (1977). Reversed facial images and the mere-exposure hypothesis. *Journal of Personality and Social Psychology,* *35*(8), 597–601. https://doi.org/10.1037/0022-3514.35.8.597

McLeod, S. A. (2018, January, 21). *Skinner - operant conditioning.* Simply Psychology. https://www.simplypsychology.org/operant-conditioning.html

Gneezy, U., Meier, S., & Rey-Biel, P. (2011). When and Why Incentives (Don't) Work to Modify Behavior. *The Journal of Economic Perspectives,* *25*(4), 191-209. Retrieved October 5, 2020, from http://www.jstor.org/stable/41337236

Harmon-Jones, E. (2000). Cognitive Dissonance and Experienced Negative Affect: Evidence that Dissonance Increases Experienced Negative Affect Even in the Absence of Aversive Consequences.

Personality and Social Psychology Bulletin, 26(12), 1490–1501. https://doi.org/10.1177/01461672002612004

Mcleod, S. (1970, January 01). Systematic Desensitization. Retrieved October 05, 2020, from https://www.simplypsychology.org/Systematic-Desensitisation.html

www.ingramcontent.com/pod-product-compliance
Lightning Source LLC
Chambersburg PA
CBHW070754300326
41914CB00053B/656